David Abramson · Bronis R. de Supinski (Eds.)

Supercomputing Frontiers

5th Asian Conference, SCFA 2019
Singapore, March 11–14, 2019
Proceedings

Editors
David Abramson
University of Queensland
St. Lucia, QLD, Australia

Bronis R. de Supinski
Lawrence Livermore National Laboratory
Livermore, CA, USA

https://doi.org/10.1007/978-3-030-18645-6

LNCS Sublibrary: SL1 – Theoretical Computer Science and General Issues

Preface

As the share of supercomputers in Asia continues to increase, the relevance of supercomputing merits a supercomputing conference for Asia. Supercomputing Asia (SCA) 2019 was an umbrella of notable supercomputing events that promote a vibrant HPC ecosystem in Asian countries and was held March 11–14, 2019, at Suntec Singapore Convention and Exhibition Centre.

The technical program of SCA 2019 had its roots in Supercomputing Frontiers (SCF), which is Singapore's annual international HPC conference that provides a platform for leaders from both academia and industry to interact and to discuss visionary ideas, important global trends, and substantial innovations in supercomputing. In March 2017, the National Supercomputing Centre (NSCC) Singapore took over hosting of Supercomputing Frontiers 2017 (SCF 2017). NSCC expanded the scope of SCF by embarking on SupercomputingAsia 2018. NSCC was established in 2015 and manages Singapore's first national petascale facility with available HPC resources to support science and engineering computing needs for academic, research, and industry communities. SCA 2018 was attended by over 800 delegates from over 24 different countries.

SCA 2019 program highlights included:

- Quantum computing
- Precision medicine
- Hyperscalers
- Green data center strategies and management
- Joint HPC Cloud Security Workshop
- HPC-AI competition
- Industry talks by leading vendors
- Technical papers and poster sessions

The co-located HPC events included:

- Asia Pacific Research Platform (APRP) Conference
- ASEAN HPC Workshop
- Conference on Next-Generation Arithmetic (CoNGA)
- Supercomputing Frontiers Asia (SCFA)
- Singapore–Japan–Australia Joint HPC Session

SCFA represents the technical program for SCA 2019, consisting of four tracks:

- Application, Algorithms, and Libraries
- Programming and System Software
- Data, Storage, and Visualization
- Architecture, Network/Communications, and Management

After rigorous peer review, we selected six papers for inclusion in the proceedings, representing an acceptance rate of 18%. These cover a range of topics including memory fault handling, linear algebra, image processing, heterogenous computing, resource usage prediction and data caching. We selected an additional eight abstracts for presentation.

We are grateful to our colleagues for submitting papers to the SCA 2019 scientific sessions, as well as to the members of the Program Committee for selecting this year's attractive program.

February 2019

David Abramson
Bronis de Supinski

Organization

David Abramson	University of Queensland, Australia
Bronis de Supinski	Lawrence Livermore National Laboratory, USA

Program Chairs

David Abramson	University of Queensland, Australia
Bronis de Supinski	Lawrence Livermore National Laboratory, USA

Program Committee

Olivier Aumage	Inria, France
Rosa M. Badia	Barcelona Supercomputing Center, Spain
Costas Bekas	IBM Research Zurich, Switzerland
Janine Bennett	Sandia National Laboratories, USA
Ron Brightwell	Sandia National Laboratories, USA
Ali Butt	Virginia Tech, USA
Sunita Chandrasekaran	University of Delaware, USA
Ewa Deelman	University of Southern California, USA
Anshu Dubey	Argonne National Laboratory, USA
Hal Finkel	Argonne National Laboratory, USA
Sandra Gesing	University of Notre Dame, USA
Bilel Hadri	KAUST, Saudi Arabia
Michael Heroux	Sandia National Laboratories, USA
Nikhil Jain	Nvidia, USA
John Kim	KAIST, South Korea
Quincey Koziol	Lawrence Berkeley National Laboratory, USA
Piotr Luszczek	University of Tenessee, USA
Arthur Maccabe	Oak Ridge National Laboratory
Naoya Maruyama	Lawrence Livermore National Laboratory, USA
Suzanne McIntosh	New York University, USA
Antonio Peña	Barcelona Supercomputing Center (BSC), Spain
Ryota Shioya	The University of Tokyo, Japan
Min Si	Argonne National Laboratory, USA
Nathan Tallent	Pacific Northwest National Laboratory, USA
Michela Taufer	University of Tennessee, USA
Weikuan Yu	Florida State University, USA
Bu Sung Lee	NTU, Singapore
Ronald Minnich	Google, USA

Contents

Practical Resource Usage Prediction Method for Large Memory Jobs in HPC Clusters

Xiuqiao Li[1(✉)], Nan Qi[1], Yuanyuan He[2], and Bill McMillan[3]

[1] IBM China Systems Laboratory, Beijing, China
{lxiuqiao,qinan}@cn.ibm.com
[2] IBM China Systems Laboratory, Xi'an, China
yyhe@cn.ibm.com
[3] IBM United Kingdom Limited, Hursley, UK
bill.mcmillan@uk.ibm.com

Abstract. Users in high performance computing (HPC) clusters normally face challenges to specify accurate resource estimates for running their applications as batch jobs. Prediction is a common way to alleviate this complexity by using historical job records of previous runs to estimate resource usage for new coming jobs. Most of existing resource prediction methods directly build a single model to consider all of the jobs in clusters. However, people in production usage tend to only focus on the resource usage of jobs with certain patterns, e.g. jobs with large memory consumption. This paper proposes a practical resource prediction method for large memory jobs. The proposed method first tries to predict whether a job tends to use large memory size, and then predicts the final memory usage using a model which is trained by only historical large memory jobs. Using several real-world job traces collected from large production clusters of IBM Spectrum LSF customer sites, the evaluation results show that the average prediction errors can be reduced up to 40% for nearly 90% of large memory jobs. Meanwhile, the model training cost can be reduced over 30% for the evaluated job traces.

Keywords: Resource usage prediction · Large memory jobs · Resource manager

1 Introduction

Nowadays high performance computing (HPC) clusters are not only deployed in large research centers, but also widely adopted by industries such as chip design and manufacture, life sciences, etc. This trend brings more diverse workload patterns to HPC clusters compared with the traditional scientific applications. As those clusters normally consists of thousands of nodes, it is common to use resource managers (e.g. IBM Spectrum LSF [1], Slurm [2], Moab [3]) to manage resources and make decisions to allocate proper resources for applications submitted by end users. Resource managers enable multiple users sharing massive cluster resources by scheduling applications as batch jobs in queue systems. However, end users generally have little knowledge of computing resources, while resource managers normally rely on accurate resource

D. Abramson and B. R. de Supinski (Eds.): SCFA 2019, LNCS 11416, pp. 1–17, 2019.
https://doi.org/10.1007/978-3-030-18645-6_1

requirements specified by users to scheduling and allocating resources. This conflict produces challenges for cluster administrators to achieve high resource utilization and job execution efficiency in their clusters. For example, when users tend to over-estimate the resource usage of their applications, resource manager will finally place fewer jobs to run in the cluster as the reserved additional resources cannot be currently used by other waiting jobs. Conversely, application may fail due to compete resources when users made under-estimation of resources usage. Another consequence of inaccurate memory requirement is wasting budget to apply excessive memory when bursting workloads to cloud, where the resources are charged by size over time [25].

Recent rapid progress on machine learning gives the opportunities to make resource managers smarter. Specifically, job resource usage together with the job submission options (e.g. submission queue, job command) are normally recorded by resource managers as accounting information after applications are completed. Applications in large production cluster are normally run repeatably. Therefore, it is possible to explore the relationship of resource usage and job patterns from historical job records. Previous work have been done for predicting job memory usage [4, 5], job runtimes [6, 7], etc. Most of those work focus on building models using all of the historical data, and comparing various machine learning algorithms on prediction accuracy.

Based on our customer experience, we found the special needs for resource prediction from with real world industry customers. Specifically, people only care about the memory usage for those large memory jobs, such as more than several or even hundreds of gigabytes. For small memory jobs, there is no need to know the memory usage in such fine-grained size compared with the massive available memory on the nodes. To satisfy this need, we propose a practical resource prediction method to improve the prediction accuracy for the large memory jobs. Considering the workload characteristics and customer needs, we mainly made the following contributions in this study:

- We analyzed the characteristics of workload traces collected from real customers, and found the number of jobs consuming large memory is smaller than small memory ones. Then we adopt the over-sampling method for large memory jobs to reduce the information loss.
- Considering both prediction accuracy and training cost, we propose a practical prediction method using two-stages prediction models. The method removes the noise of small memory jobs when predict the final memory usage. As training complexity is reduced with smaller number of jobs and class number, it is suitable for scenarios with high model updating frequency.
- We performed evaluation tests using the collected job traces, and analyzed the benefits of the proposed method in reducing prediction errors for large memory jobs and accelerating model training.

The rest of the paper starts with Sect. 2 which gives the motivation of this work by summarizing the characteristics of real-world job traces, and then lists the main design goals of this paper. In Sects. 3 and 4, we introduce the specific work need to be done during dataset preparation, and the proposed two-stage prediction method for large memory jobs. Evaluation results are analyzed in Sect. 5, and Sect. 6 summarized related work on job resource usage prediction. At last, we make the conclusions and introduce the future directions in Sect. 7.

2 Motivation

The work in this paper is motivated from real-world scenarios encountered by resource manager users. In this section, we will first introduce the analysis of job traces collected from our customers. Then the design goals of the resource prediction method is given based on the analysis results.

2.1 Real-World Traces Analysis

IBM Spectrum LSF is widely used in large scale computing centers from academic research centers to industrial datacenters and even on cloud. The largest clusters in those sites consists of several and even ten thousand of computing nodes with millions of jobs finished per day. We collected three job traces from those sites[1] and had surveys with the cluster administrators about the job patterns in those clusters. Based on our experiences and analysis of real job traces in their clusters, we have the following major observations:

- ***Large memory jobs are only small portions of the whole job records though contribute to most of the total memory consumptions.***

Table 1 shows that the statistics of total memory usage of large and small memory jobs. Take Trace A as an example, 99.49% of total memory usage are contributed by 37.3% of jobs consuming memory larger than 1 GB. Trace C has more large memory jobs but most of them use less than 16 GB memory, while the large memory jobs of the other two traces are scattered between 1 GB and 128 GB.

Table 1. Job and memory usage statistics of job traces by per-job memory usage (>1 GB as large memory jobs and others as small memory jobs).

Traces	#Jobs	Small memory jobs (%)	Small memory usage (%)	Large memory jobs (%)	Large memory usage (%)
Trace A	587k	62.7	0.51	37.3	99.49
Trace B	907k	77	3.3	23	96.7
Trace C	1m	43.4	12.1	56.6	87.9

- ***Cluster administrators care more about the accuracy of memory usage of large memory jobs.***

Figure 1(a) shows the job traces statistics of user specified errors compared with real memory usage consumption. The relative user specified error of a job is calculated as the following formula:

$$100 * |User\_Specified\_Mem - Real\_Mem\_Usage| / Real\_Mem\_Usage \quad (1)$$

[1] The customer related information in the job traces are hidden in this paper due to IBM data privacy policies.

As there are no user specified memory values recorded in Trace B, we just show the statistics of Trace A and C. The absolute value of memory loss has large impact on cluster resource utilizations. For example, it is a common case that a chip design simulation application can consume hundreds of gigabytes memory in maximum. Meanwhile, end users specify several times of real memory usage to guarantee application running correctly. That means hundreds of gigabytes are wasted and cannot be concurrently used by other jobs.

In contrast, Fig. 1(b) shows that the small memory jobs tend to be completed in short time even in a minute. It could be tolerable to have certain user specified errors for those small memory jobs. One exception is there are lots of small memory jobs run for over 1 h and less than 6 h in Trace C. Those jobs are possibly compute-intensive jobs, and we found the user specified errors are quite low for those jobs.

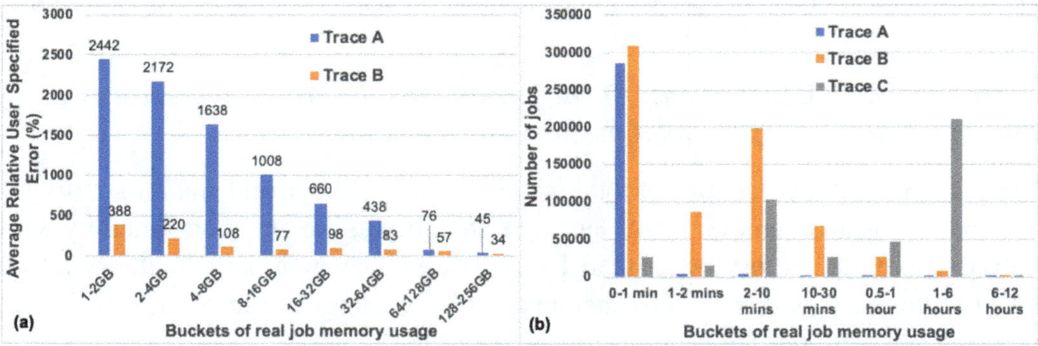

Fig. 1. Job traces statistics: (a) User specified errors for job memory usage; (b) Number of small memory jobs by their job runtime ranges

- ***Small memory jobs introduce noises in predicting memory usage for large memory jobs***

Figure 2 shows that the comparisons of memory usage prediction errors for large memory jobs using datasets with different amount of small memory jobs. It can be observed that the prediction is more accurate with a smaller number of small memory jobs in the training datasets. It is easy to be explained as the small memory jobs become noise data points when training model for large memory jobs.

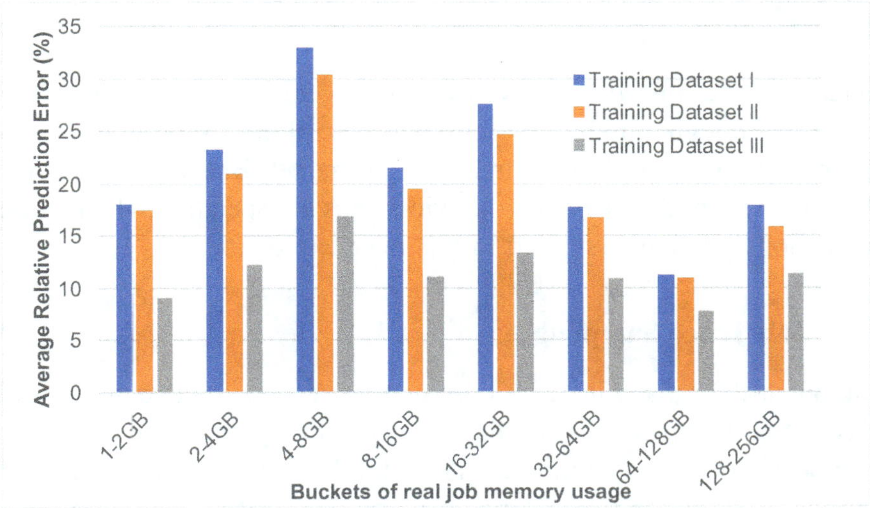

Fig. 2. Comparison of the average relative prediction errors of job memory usage by using training datasets (generated from job trace A) with various portions of small memory jobs: Dataset I consists of all jobs, Dataset II has large memory jobs and half part of small memory jobs, and Dataset III only contains of large memory jobs.

- ***Jobs with new job patterns keep updating during the cluster is running***

According to our analysis of those traces, there are always new job patterns cannot fit into the ones recognized using previous job records. Cluster administrators explain this observation as there are new projects started with new applications or people improve their work by changing their applications or scripts. That means the prediction model needs to be updated more frequently to include the new job patterns. Considering the large amount of historical jobs in the training datasets, the training model tasks are quite time-consuming. Resource prediction face challenges to have low training cost while keeping good prediction accuracy at the same time.

2.2 Design Goals

To satisfy the above real scenarios faced by resource managers, we target to design a practical resource prediction method using machine learning models for large memory jobs. The method can help resource manager administrators to better adjust over-estimated user specified memory values for their large memory jobs, improve the overall cluster utilization for memory resource and save budget of applying cloud resources to burst workloads.

Specifically, the method aims to achieve the following design goals: (1) to improve the memory usage prediction accuracy for large memory jobs with high coverage rate; (2) to reduce the model training cost to support frequent model updating; (3) to keep low prediction latency to reduce the impact on job submission performance.

3 Dataset Preparation

The collected job traces need to be well pre-processed before using for building prediction models. Enough number of job-related attributes should be extracted and mapped to input training features to train a good model. Besides the normal machine learning flow to prepare datasets, the following steps are specific to the requirements of large memory jobs prediction studied in this paper.

3.1 Biased Job Trace Sampling

It is a common case for many industrial production clusters to have millions of finished jobs per day. The training cost of building a daily updating model using months of data would be impossible. Data sampling is one of the feasible ways to reduce the training dataset size while keeps the job patterns as many as possible. Based on the job traces analysis, there are normally more small memory jobs though the total memory usage cannot be comparable with the one of large memory jobs. Therefore, the large memory jobs could be overwhelmed if we adopt uniform sampling method to extract training datasets. Instead, the large memory jobs need to be favored than other ones during sampling.

3.2 Job Attributes Extraction

The job traces are log based formats which contains the job submission options together with the job resource usage information. Some log fields are directly readable, while some other fields are encoded with rich information. Generally, resource managers provide public APIs to decode detail attributes from those encoded fields.

- The encoded job option fields are generally using bit flags to record multiple boolean options (e.g. whether a job is an interactive or urgent one).
- Some job fields need to be further processed to extract useful information. For example, the job submission time is normally recorded as Unix time which cannot be directly used as a feature. It is more meaningful to extract day or hour in a week or a day to recognize the time related job submission patterns, such as a user may always run his simulation application before leaving office every day.
- There are also more customized job fields which need to be processed as multiple features. For example, people may leverage job names or project names to 'tag' some job specific information with pre-defined formats.

We directly extracted 30+ features (e.g. queue, project, application, job group names, job command, requested resource names and their values) from the collected job traces used by the work in this paper. The features with non-integer data types are encoded into integers and normalized before used to training models. It is possible to further extract more useful information, but it is not the scope of the main problem addressed in this paper (Table 2).

Table 2. Training features extracted for the studies in this paper.

Feature	Data type	Feature	Data type
Submission User ID	*Integer*	*Attached SLA Name*	*String*
Submission User Group	*String*	*Submission Host Name*	*String*
Queue Name	*String*	*Input File Name*	*String*
Application Profile Name	*String*	*Output File Name*	*String*
Project Name	*String*	*Specified Job Begin Time*	*Date*
Job Command Name	*String*	*Specified Termination Time*	*Data*
Job Working Directory	*String*	*Job Name*	*String*
Resource Requirements	*String*	*Pre-execution Command Name*	*String*
Requested Number of Slots	*Integer*	*Job Group Name*	*String*
User Login Shell	*String*	*User Specified Memory Reservation Value*	*Integer*
Job Submission Working Directory	*String*	*Job Description*	*String*
Advanced Reservation Name	*String*	*Array Job or Single Job*	*Boolean*
License Project Name	*String*	*Post-execution Command Name*	*String*
Job Submission Day of Week	*Integer*	*Job Submission Hour of Day*	*Integer*
Job Options	*Integer*	*User Specified Runtime Limit or Estimation*	*Integer*

3.3 Abnormal Job Removal

Jobs could be terminated from the system before normal completion. For example, user or administrator may explicitly kill the job submitted with wrong options. Also, application may run into errors and terminate itself with certain exit codes. Those incomplete jobs surely become the noise points when training model. We remove the jobs with following abnormal cases from our job traces.

- Jobs with zero or minus memory usage
- Jobs with zero or minus runtimes
- Jobs finished with exit status or exit codes

Besides, we follow other standard feature engineering steps [18] to further refine the features, such as feature encoding (e.g. mapping the value of string type fields as integer values) and normalization.

4 Resource Prediction Method

In this section, we present the design of the proposed resource prediction method for large memory jobs. The key idea of our method is to separate the mode training as two stages: firstly, a binary classification model is built to determine whether a job will consume large or small memory; then a regression model is trained by just using the

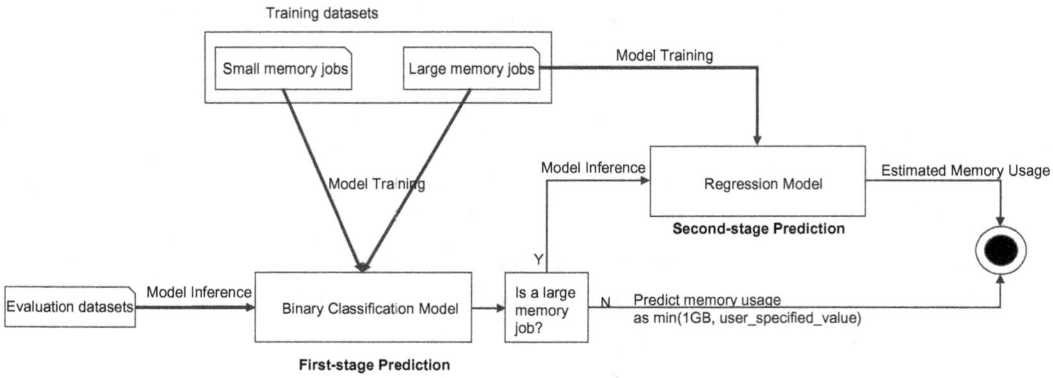

Fig. 3. Proposed prediction flow for job memory usage

historical large memory jobs to predict the final memory usage for the jobs which are predicted to use large memory. Figure 3 describes the overall prediction flow with the above method.

4.1 Predicting Job Memory Usage Type

Predicting the correct job memory usage is not easy, but the complexity of predicting whether a job tend to belong a large or small memory one can be significantly reduced. The latter one becomes a binary classification problem, while the former one is a multi-class classification problem or a regression problem. We treat the job with memory usage larger than 1 GB as large memory one in this paper. However, this boundary could be dynamically changed in production system based on the practical workload needs.

As shown in Fig. 3, the prediction accuracy of this binary classification model needs to be very high to reduce the number of wrongly predicted large memory jobs got requeued at runtimes. Besides adopting biased sampling to increase the number of large memory jobs in the training datasets, it is important to extract the user specified memory usage as an input feature. Though people tend to specify much bigger memory value for their jobs, this value gives some clues on whether a job will use large memory or not. For example, user may specify always 4 GB as the reserved memory size for their small memory jobs, while specify a few hundred GB of memory size for large memory jobs. Combining this value with the real job memory usage, the model could possibly infer another job from the same user with 4 GB memory requirements as a small memory job.

While there are standard metrics (e.g. precision, recall) to evaluate the classification performance, we define two evaluation metrics to better correlate with the context of our work. Specifically, we define ***coverage rate (CR)*** and ***incorrect coverage rate (ICR)*** to separately quantify the percentage of large memory jobs which got correct prediction (*Hit_LMEM_Jobs*), and the percentage of small memory jobs which are wrongly classified as large memory ones (*Miss_SMEM_Jobs*). The calculation formulas are as follows. Therefore, the prediction target is to achieve higher coverage rate while keeps incorrect coverage rate as lower as possible.

$$CR = \#Hit\_LMEM\_Jobs/\#Total\_LMEM\_Jobs \quad (2)$$

$$ICR = \#Miss\_SMEM\_Jobs/\#Total\_SMEM\_Jobs \quad (3)$$

The classification version of random forester method is chosen as the binary classification algorithm to train the first stage model. We also did basic hyper-parameter search using the public random search method provided by *scikit-learn* toolkits [19].

4.2 Predicting Large Job Memory Usage

As long as the large memory jobs have been identified with the first stage model, it becomes straightforward to train another model by just using the historical large memory jobs. The results given by Fig. 2 show that such model can remove the noises of small memory jobs and get better prediction accuracy. We use the regression version of random forest algorithm in *scikit-learn* toolkits to train the large memory model.

Meanwhile, as the number of jobs in the training datasets is reduced, the model training time can also be significantly shortened. Though now we need to build two models, the training time of the first stage model is much shorter than training a regression or multi-class classification model using all large and small jobs. The total time of training two models is also shorter than the one of training a single model.

Furthermore, as there is no dependency between the models in two stages, model training can be concurrently started with additional hardware resources. Then the training time can be further reduced by hiding the latency. We will show more comparison results in the following evaluation section.

4.3 Tolerate Incorrect Predictions

Prediction always have errors and the more important thing is how to minimize the impact of incorrect predictions. Specific to our predictions, we have the following prediction errors during the two different stages.

- *Predict a large memory job as using small amount of memory*: this job will not get memory usage prediction, and resource manager will reserve memory if user specified memory requirement. Otherwise, the job will compete memory resource with other jobs at the run time. The former one may waste memory but can be acceptable if the percentage of missing rate is low. The latter one may encounter memory failures, and can be requeued to run again depending on resource manager configurations.
- *Predict a small memory job as using large amount of memory*: this job will get a memory size which is larger than its consumption. As this kind of jobs tend to have short duration, there will be not much impact on overall memory utilization.
- *Memory prediction is under-estimated by the second stage model*: in practical, administrator can round up the predicted value to the memory bucket upper value. Then the impact introduced by this kind of under-estimation errors can be reduced.

4.4 Model Inference for New Jobs

Finally, the trained model will be used for predicting job memory usage for new coming jobs. Compared with single model approach, our method requires up to two inference operations to get final memory predictions. However, the time granularity of job submission latency is quite larger than model inference latency. It has little impact on the job submission throughput. In addition, one can also perform inference from the two models at the same time with certain probability. Then the inference latency can be hidden as one longest latency of the two models.

5 Evaluation Results and Analysis

In this section, we introduce the evaluation details of proposed method using the traces we described in Sect. 3. We will first describe the testing environments and strategy, then prove the benefits of our prediction method in terms of prediction accuracy, model training and inference efficiency.

5.1 Experimental Setup

IBM Spectrum LSF Predictor [21] is a tool to predict job resource metrics using LSF job traces. We used this tool to implement and evaluate proposed prediction method for large memory jobs in this paper. The tool is running as a Docker container and includes the steps of a complete machine learning flow. The testbed is a X86_64 machine with 44 Intel Xeon E5 CPUs, and 64 GB physical memory.

We used three real world job traces collected from IBM Spectrum LSF customers for the evaluation tests. Besides the job memory size statistics information in Sect. 2, more statistics information is listed in Table 3. Note we used biased sampling for large

Table 3. Statistics of job traces used for evaluation tests.

Metrics	Trace A	Trace B	Trace C
Time periods of job traces (days)	36	4	4
Num. of total jobs	587k	907k	1m
Num. of active users	1270	3085	506
Num. of projects	5589	278	23
Num. of jobs in training/evaluation datasets	469.6k/117.4k	700k/207k	750k/251.5k
Num. of large/small memory jobs in training dataset	175.3k/294.3k	538k/162k	428.8k/321.2k
Num. of large/small memory jobs in evaluation dataset	43.7k/73.7k	47k/115k	183.6/137.6k
Avg. large/small job memory usage (GB)	28.83/0.155	7.46/0.29	2.54/0.43
Avg. runtimes of large/small memory jobs (mins)	175.56/16.6	92/12	221/103

memory jobs to generate Trace A from the original traces, which can retain the job patterns over long periods.

We split roughly 80% of jobs as training datasets, while use the left jobs as inference datasets. The evaluation experiments do comparison tests between single model method and the two-stage model proposed in this paper. To make fair comparisons, we used the same hyper-parameter settings to predict the memory usage for both two kinds of prediction methods. Table 4 shows the configurations for the Random Forest algorithms used by the single model and our two-stages model approaches. To accelerate the model training, we configure *n_jobs* as 10 to run training in parallel across multiple CPUs. The following sections will give the detail analysis of comparisons in different metrics.

Table 4. Hyper-parameter settings for model trainings.

Hyper-parameter	Single model	1st stage model	2nd stage model
n_estimators	100	50	100
n_jobs	10	10	10
max_depth	Auto	Auto	Auto
random_state	2	2	2
max_features	Auto	Auto	Auto

5.2 Prediction Accuracy and Efficiency

This section first analyzes the prediction accuracy of first stage model in distinguishing large and small memory jobs. Then we evaluate the prediction errors of job memory usage for large memory jobs using the second stage model.

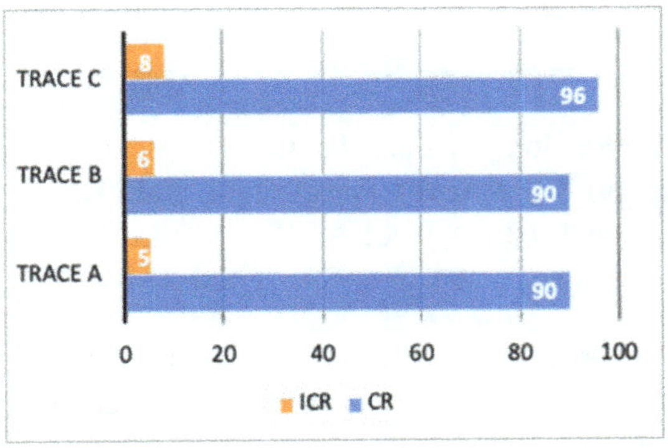

Fig. 4. Coverage rate (CR) and Incorrect coverage rate (ICR) of three job traces

Figure 4 shows the *CR* and *ICR* of three tested job traces produced by random forest binary classification model. We can see over 90% of large memory jobs can get correct prediction for their memory usage types, while only less than 8% of small memory jobs are wrongly predicted. Trace C even can correctly predict 90% of large memory jobs. This result provides a good basis for the second stage prediction, which finally predict the memory usage for the large memory jobs recognized by the binary classification model in the first stage.

For those wrongly predicted large memory jobs, it is possible that those jobs may fail to get enough memory during runtime. Jobs may suffer from the overhead of memory swapping or even encounter execution failure. On one hand, the prediction quality of classification model can be further tuned to get better prediction accuracy. Note that we don't perform too much tuning efforts on the feature engineering and model hyper-parameter tuning in this paper. Therefore, it can be expected that the CR value can possibly be further increased, while the ICR value can be reduced to filter more small memory jobs from the second prediction stage. One the other hand, resource managers can make smart allocation adjustments once a job exceeds its predicted memory size. For example, the job can be checkpointed and migrated to other hosts or simply requeued to be rescheduled with the user specified memory size. As we can achieve pretty higher classification predictions, the overall memory utilizations still can be significantly improved even small number of jobs needs to be restarted.

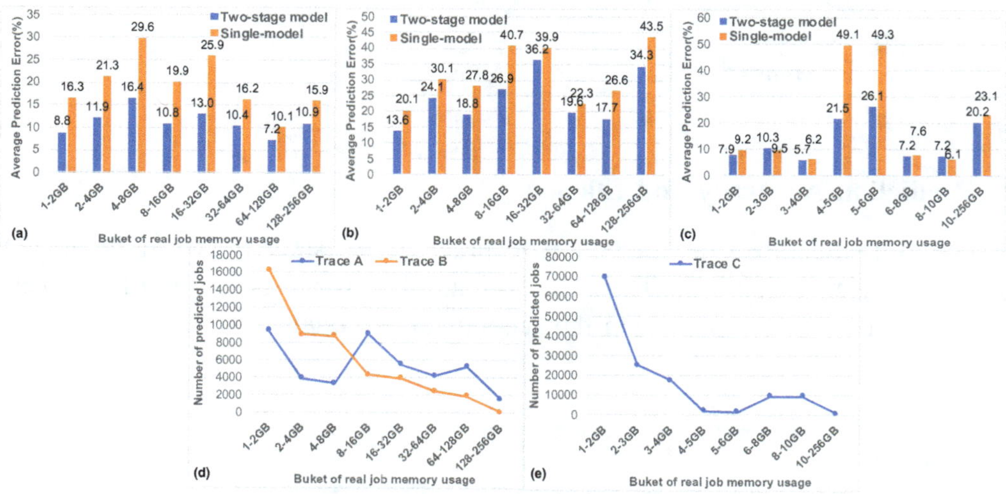

Fig. 5. Comparisons of prediction accuracy between single model (baseline) and two-stage model (proposed method): (a) Trace A; (b) Trace B; (c) Trace C, and distribution of predicted jobs by job memory usage buckets: (d) Trace A&B; (e) Trace C

Figure 5(a–c) shows the prediction accuracy comparisons between existing single model approach and proposed two-stages prediction method. To fairly evaluate the improvements, the figures draw the calculated average prediction errors of each pre-defined memory usage buckets for the large memory jobs recognized by the first-stage model. The prediction error numbers are marked on the top of each bar in the figure. We try to split the job memory usage buckets with roughly balanced number of jobs in each bucket. So the bucket distribution in Trace C is different with the other two traces as most of its jobs have memory usage less than 16 GB.

Figure 5(d) and (e) depicts the number of jobs in each bucket for the three traces. From the results, we can see obvious improvements on prediction errors for all of the three traces with the proposed method. The average percentages of improvements for Trace A, B and C are 40.7, 24.3 and 14.5 respectively. The results prove the advantages of removing the noises of small memory jobs from the training model. Although there are a little bit increments of prediction errors for the buckets 2–3 GB and 8–10 GB of Trace C, the prediction error numbers are less than 10% and can be tolerated in practice. It might be related the particular unknown job patterns in those two buckets, which can be further investigated. We don't see this phenomenon in other two traces.

Furthermore, the predictions improvements compared with single model approach can save corresponding percentage of bucket to use cloud resources when moving those workloads to public cloud. Take the jobs of Trace A with 1–2 GB requirements as an example, the average improvements of prediction errors can be reduced by nearly 50%. That means the cluster must apply a VM with 2 GB memory (e.g. *t3.small* from AWS [24]) to run the job, but now only needs to provision a VM with 1 GB memory (e.g. *t3.micro*) for the job. As the price shown by AWS, the cost reduces from $0.0208 per hour to $0.0104 per hour. As shown by Fig. 1, user specified errors of memory requirements could be hundreds to thousands of times compared with real usage. The proposed approach in this paper can significantly reduce the budget of moving workloads to cloud in large scale clusters.

In summary, the proposed two-stages prediction method is much better than building a single model to predict memory usage for large memory jobs. As the first stage model can get good coverage rate for identifying large memory jobs, it is practical and effective to use the second model with only historical large memory jobs for final prediction.

5.3 Model Training Cost Analysis

Figure 6 shows the evaluation results of model training efficiency. As there are two models needed to be built in our proposed method, the left figure gives the distribution of training time of the two models, and the training time numbers (seconds) are marked in the corresponding bars. Also, the green bars in the figure show the training time numbers of building a single model. We can see the cost of building the first stage binary classification model is much lower than building a regression model using the same datasets. Meanwhile, as the second stage model only needs to train the large memory jobs, the model building time can also be significantly reduced. That proves that the total training cost can be reduced even we split the model training into two stages. This observation can be further confirmed by the improvement percentage of training time compared with the training time of single model in Fig. 6(b).

As we introduced in Sect. 4.2, the two stage models have no building dependency and can be trained concurrently with additional computing resources. Figure 6(b) shows the improvements of training the two stage models in serial or parallel. The percentage numbers are marked above the corresponding bars. For both two cases, the proposed method requires less training cost to build those models. As the problem complexity is increased by the number of jobs in training datasets, we believe the

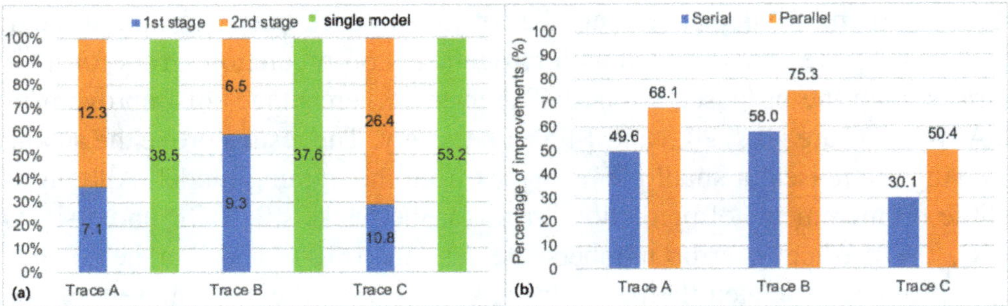

Fig. 6. Comparisons of model training cost: (a) training time distributions of two stages models and single model; (b) percentage of training time improvements compared between single model training (baseline) and two stages models training (including both total training time of running two models sequentially and in parallel)

improvements can be further enlarged when training large models containing long periods of historical job records.

5.4 Model Inference Performance

One potential side effect of using two-stage models is the inference latency may be increased compared with predicting using a single model. Tables 5 and 6 show the statistics of model inference latency and total inference time. We can see the inference latency from the second stage model is increased. The reason should be that there are more computing efforts of fitting a large memory value. However, as the inference latency is only microseconds level, it is pretty little impact on the job submission performance in practical. Generally, submitting a job to resource manager requires setup connections to remote master daemon, process requests and create persistence

Table 5. Comparisons of model inference latencies

Trace Name	Avg. model inference latency (microseconds)		
	1st stage	2nd stage	Single model
Trace A	2.38	7.28	4.88
Trace B	1.57	7.31	2.87
Trace C	1.76	4.49	3.04

Table 6. Comparisons of total time of model inference for jobs in the evaluation datasets

Trace Name	Total time of model inference (milliseconds)			Inference delay (percent)
	1st stage	2nd stage	Single model	
Trace A	279.6	318.2	597.8	4.38
Trace B	325.3	343.7	595.9	12.3
Trace C	442.8	618.2	765.7	38.6

entry by resource managers. So, the job submission latency of a single job is around several or dozens of milliseconds. Compared with the network and resource manager processing delay, the inference latency of predicting job resource usage can be totally ignored. In addition, there are lots of work on using GPUs to do model inference, which can significantly accelerate the floating computing operations [22, 23].

6 Related Work

Using machine learning algorithms to predict job resource usage is one of the hottest topics in recent years, and a lot of research work has been done on not only memory usage prediction, but also CPU usage, job wall time predictions, etc.

Many works have been done on directly predicting the value of job resource usage [4, 5]. The predicted value then can be integrated by resource managers to help users or administrators to adjust incorrect specified usage value. Taghavi [4] et al. from Qualcomm introduced their work on predicting job memory usage using various machine learning algorithms and tools. Their work shows the memory usage of prior jobs can be good guess for next jobs, and a simple linear regression model can be used for prediction. Another IBM research team [5] performed similar work on using various machine learning algorithms (e.g. k-NN, Random forest, SVM) to do memory usage prediction using LSF job trace records. Those work provides good basis for our study in this paper, and proves the feasibility of using machine learning models to predict further job memory usage. However, instead of building a single model using all of collected data, we target to only predict job memory usage more accurately for large memory jobs using two-stage prediction method. Administrator don't put too much attention on small memory usage due to the fact of its short job duration and massive memory on modern computing nodes. Therefore, our work is more practical for production usage and promote the prediction accuracy for those jobs really cared by resource manager users.

Besides memory usage prediction, a lot of other researchers focus on predicting more other job related metrics, such as job runtimes [6, 7, 10, 11], job queue-waiting time [12, 13], job start times [20], job completion time [14], power usage [16, 17], etc. Instead of using job submission records, some of the work are directly using the recent previous runs of the same applications to calculate the runtimes for next jobs, which limited to certain suitable scenarios. While our work focuses on predicting memory usage for large memory jobs, it could potentially be extended to more broader scenarios. For example, people may also care about the resource usage of long running jobs. Then it is also applicable to do similar two-stage prediction models for better prediction accuracy.

Differ with predicting the usage value, there are lots of work investigating how to binary classification can do some correctness judgements in cluster or job usage. Guo et al. [8] proposed to predict whether user specified runtime limits are under-estimated compared with actual job runtimes. Then user can be notified to correct their job limit and ensure job not being terminated unexpectedly. Andresen et al. [9] used classification algorithms to do similar predictions on whether a job will fail due to resource shortage. Their work also performed regression models to predict memory usage and job runtimes. One innovation of their approach is that they introduced additional per-user features like average memory usage, requested memory and runtimes to train the models. In our paper, we also use binary classification models to identify the large memory jobs in the first stage prediction model.

7 Conclusions and Future Work

Resource managers can perform better job scheduling decisions and overall cluster resource utilization with more accurate job resource requirements. In hybrid cloud environments, accurate memory predictions can also save lots of budget to burst workloads to cloud, which is one of popular use patterns adopted by HPC sites. We analyzed the real customer scenarios and found that administrators have more emphasis on the memory usage of large memory jobs. Instead of building a single model using all of historical jobs, we conducted evaluation tests using real world customer job traces to demonstrate that a two-stage prediction approach can remove the noise of small memory jobs and promote the prediction accuracy of large memory jobs with a high coverage rate. The proposed prediction method is suitable for the practical usage to predict job memory usage in production systems.

In the future, we plan to collect more large-scale job traces to further evaluate the benefits on prediction quality and performance. Also, we believe the job memory usage prediction of large memory jobs is only one of the practical scenarios to adopt the two-stage prediction method. In the next steps, we will evaluate whether it is useful to have better prediction for the job runtimes of long running jobs in HPC clusters.

References

1. IBM Spectrum LSF. www.ibm.com/Storage/LSF. Accessed 01 Jan 2019
2. Slurm Workload Manager. https://slurm.schedmd.com/. Accessed 01 Jan 2019
3. Moab Cloud HPC Suite. www.adaptivecomputing.com/moab-hpc-basic-edition/. Accessed 01 Jan 2019
4. Taghavi, T., Lupetini, M., Kretchmer, Y.: Compute job memory recommender system using machine learning. In: Proceedings of the 22nd ACM SIGKDD International Conference on Knowledge Discovery and Data Mining (KDD 2016), pp. 609–616. ACM, New York (2016)
5. Rodrigues, E.R., Cunha, R.L., Netto, M.A., Spriggs, M.: Helping HPC users specify job memory requirements via machine learning. In: Proceedings of the Third International Workshop on HPC User Support Tools, pp. 6–13. IEEE Press (2016)
6. Yang, L.T., Ma, X., Mueller, F.: Cross-platform performance prediction of parallel applications using partial execution. In: Proceedings of the 2005 ACM/IEEE Conference on Supercomputing (2005)
7. Gaussier, E., Glesser, D., Reis, V., Trystram, D.: Improving backfilling by using machine learning to predict running times. In: Proceedings of the International Conference for High Performance Computing, Networking, Storage and Analysis, p. 64. ACM (2015)
8. Guo, J., Nomura, A., Barton, R., Zhang, H., Matsuoka, S.: Machine learning predictions for underestimation of job runtime on HPC system. In: Yokota, R., Wu, W. (eds.) SCFA 2018. LNCS, vol. 10776, pp. 179–198. Springer, Cham (2018). https://doi.org/10.1007/978-3-319-69953-0_11

9. Andresen, D., Hsu, W., Yang, H., Okanlawon, A.: Machine learning for predictive analytics of compute cluster jobs. In: The 16th International Conference on Scientific Computing (2018, accepted)
10. Carlos, F.G.: Improving HPC applications scheduling with predictions based on automatically-collected historical data. Master thesis, UPC (2014)
11. Matsunaga, A., Fortes, J.A.: On the use of machine learning to predict the time and resources consumed by applications. In: Proceedings of the 2010 10th IEEE/ACM International Conference on Cluster, Cloud and Grid Computing, pp. 495–504. IEEE Computer Society (2010)
12. Carvalho, A., Belo, O.: Predicting waiting time in customer queuing systems. In: 2016 IEEE International Conference on Knowledge Engineering and Applications (ICKEA), pp. 155–159. IEEE Computer Society (2016)
13. Smith, W., Taylor, V., Foster, I.: Using run-time predictions to estimate queue wait times and improve scheduler performance. In: Feitelson, D.G., Rudolph, L. (eds.) JSSPP 1999. LNCS, vol. 1659, pp. 202–219. Springer, Heidelberg (1999). https://doi.org/10.1007/3-540-47954-6_11
14. Chen, X., Lu, C.-D., et al.: Predicting job completion times using system logs in supercomputing clusters. In: DSN Workshops. IEEE Computer Society (2013)
15. Storlie, C., Sexton, J., Pakin, S., et al.: AI Modeling and predicting power consumption of high performance computing jobs. preprint arXiv:1412.5247 (2014)
16. Borghesi, A., Bartolini, A., Lombardi, M., Milano, M., Benini, L.: Predictive modeling for job power consumption in HPC systems. In: Kunkel, J.M., Balaji, P., Dongarra, J. (eds.) ISC High Performance 2016. LNCS, vol. 9697, pp. 181–199. Springer, Cham (2016). https://doi.org/10.1007/978-3-319-41321-1_10
17. Author, F., Author, S.: Title of a proceedings paper. In: Editor, F., Editor, S. (eds.) CONFERENCE 2016. LNCS, vol. 9999, pp. 1–13. Springer, Heidelberg (2016)
18. Zheng, A., Casari, A.: Feature Engineering for Machine Learning - Principles and Techniques for Data Scientists. O'Reilly Media, Sebastopol (2018)
19. scikit-learn: machine learning in Python. https://scikit-learn.org. Accessed 10 Nov 2018
20. Li, H., Groep, D.L., et al.: Predicting job start times on clusters. In: IEEE/ACM International Symposium on Cluster Computing and the Grid (CCGrid), pp. 301–308. IEEE Computer Society (2004)
21. A Crystal Ball for HPC. https://www.hpcwire.com/solution_content/ibm/cross-industry/a-crystal-ball-for-hpc. Accessed 10 Dec 2018
22. GPU-Based Deep Learning Inference. https://www.nvidia.com/content/tegra/embedded-systems/pdf/jetson_tx1_whitepaper.pdf. Accessed 13 Oct 2018
23. Gardner, J.R., Pleiss, G., Bindel, D., et al.: GPyTorch: Blackbox Matrix-Matrix Gaussian Process Inference with GPU Acceleration. NeurIPS 2018. preprint arXiv:1809.11165 (2018)
24. Amazon EC2 Pricing. https://aws.amazon.com/ec2/pricing/on-demand/. Accessed 07 Feb 2019
25. IBM Spectrum LSF Hybrid Cloud. https://github.com/IBMSpectrumComputing/lsf-hybrid-cloud. Accessed 07 Feb 2019

A Crystal/Clear Pipeline for Applied Image Processing

Christopher J. Watkins[1(✉)], Nicholas Rosa[2], Thomas Carroll[3], David Ratcliffe[4], Marko Ristic[2], Christopher Russell[5], Rongxin Li[6], Vincent Fazio[7], and Janet Newman[2]

[1] Scientific Computing, Commonwealth Scientific and Industrial Research Organisation, Clayton, VIC 3181, Australia
chris.watkins@csiro.au

[2] Manufacturing, Commonwealth Scientific and Industrial Research Organisation, Clayton, VIC 3181, Australia
{nick.rosa,marko.ristic,janet.newman}@csiro.au

[3] The University of Melbourne, Parkville, VIC 3052, Australia
t.carroll4@student.unimelb.edu.au

[4] Data61, Commonwealth Scientific and Industrial Research Organisation, Acton, ACT 2601, Australia
david.ratcliffe@csiro.au

[5] Scientific Computing, Commonwealth Scientific and Industrial Research Organisation, Alexandria, NSW 1435, Australia
christopher.russell@csiro.au

[6] Data61, Commonwealth Scientific and Industrial Research Organisation, Marsfield, NSW 2122, Australia
ron.li@csiro.au

[7] Minerals, Commonwealth Scientific and Industrial Research Organisation, Clayton, VIC 3181, Australia
vincent.fazio@csiro.au

Abstract. Many long-standing image processing problems in applied science domains are finding solutions through the application of deep learning approaches to image processing. Here we present one such application; the case of classifying images of protein crystallisation droplets. The Collaborative Crystallisation Centre in Melbourne, Australia is a medium throughput service facility that produces between five and twenty thousand images per day. This submission outlines a reliable and robust machine learning pipeline that autonomously classifies these images using CSIRO's high-performance computing facilities. Our pipeline achieves improved accuracies over existing implementations and delivers these results in real time. We discuss the specific tools and techniques used to construct the pipeline, as well as the methodologies for testing and validating externally developed classification models.

Keywords: Machine learning · Deep learning · Crystallisation image · Image processing · Automation · Classification

D. Abramson and B. R. de Supinski (Eds.): SCFA 2019, LNCS 11416, pp. 19–37, 2019.
https://doi.org/10.1007/978-3-030-18645-6_2

1 Introduction

Knowing the shape of an object reveals much about its function: a single glimpse of a Ferrari and a bus allows one to predict quite accurately which vehicle would go faster. Similarly, given a high-resolution picture of a biological molecule (e.g. a protein molecule) a biologist can tell much about how it works. X-ray crystallography is the only technique that can generate very high-resolution pictures of molecules - pinpointing positions of individual atoms within a large complex molecule [10]. This technique, X-ray crystallography, is the basis for modern drug discovery, synthetic biology and indeed any field - academic or commercial - where understanding biology down to the atomic level is important. To generate an X-ray picture, a *crystal* of the biological molecule is bathed in a powerful beam of X-rays [7]. Production of the crystal samples used in X-ray crystallography is the *limiting* step in 'seeing' biology, and thus understanding it. Figure 1 illustrates the crystallography pipeline in structural biology.

Fig. 1. Structural biology pipeline. Obtaining a crystallised protein is just the beginning. Once a crystal has been grown it is irradiated with X-rays (often at a synchrotron light source). The diffraction images produced at the synchrotron are then used to calculate the atomic structure of the protein.

Crystals of proteins suitable for X-ray analysis are *notoriously difficult* to produce [17]. For each protein, hundreds or sometimes thousands of experiments are set up, where the protein sample is mixed with different cocktails of chemicals in an unsophisticated trial-and-error approach to identify conditions under which the protein will crystallise [30]. Crystal growth is a time-dependent (and intrinsically stochastic) process, so that the trials have to be examined repeatedly over a time-frame of many weeks, with the knowledge that trials that could support crystal growth may not show any crystals, due to the inherent randomness of crystal nucleation. Crystal growth of proteins, or indeed simple molecules like table salt, require that the solution becomes supersaturated and that nucleation occurs. Given supersaturation of a protein solution, the most likely outcome is the formation of a disordered precipitate. Sometimes the crystallisation trial will result in phase separation, and sometimes supersaturation is simply not achieved, and the droplet remains clear. For each of the basic classes of outcome: crystals, phase separation and precipitation there is a huge variation in the type and extent of the outcome. Even in the clear class, where the drop is unchanged, extraneous matter - dust, for example, can give a drop that has features, which are not part of the intended experiment. Further, there are no clear boundaries between the classes - for example, a clear droplet is very hard to distinguish from one with a light precipitate. Often, many outcomes can be seen in the same experiment, see Fig. 2.

The last two decades have seen the application of automation to protein crystallisation experiments - enabling more experiments to be set up, and allowing for the automatic imaging of the experiments. The relative ease of setting up experiments (and the subsequent explosion in the number of experiments created) has made human interpretation of the results unsustainable; even a human annotation of all images containing crystals is becoming increasingly rare, let alone annotation of all the non-crystal outcomes. The high-throughput Collaborative Crystallisation Centre (C3) in Melbourne, Australia has been in operation for over a decade, and has 100 or so active users at any given time. Since its inception in 2006 the C3 has built up a collection of almost 50 million visible light images of the > 3.9 million crystallisation experiments set up; 5–20 thousand new images are collected daily. Less than 5% of the C3 images have been annotated by hand.

Statistics gathered by Structural Genomics initiatives and other studies [32] have suggested that only a small percentage of initial crystallisation experiments produce diffraction quality crystals, and most useful crystals are grown by optimising near misses identified in the initial screening. Although it is widely recognised that there must be useful information that can be garnered from the trials that did not produce crystals, there are no widely available, broadly applicable methods for extracting this information. The paucity of headway in gleaning information from the experiments which fail to yield crystals can be attributed to three factors - incomplete/noisy data about how the trials were set up, incomplete/noisy data about the output of crystallisation trials, and the lack of a clear way of correlating these first two factors, although the value of this type of analysis has been long recognised [13]. The first issue - the problem of defining the crystallisation experiment relies on the development and adoption of standard vocabularies for describing crystallisation experiments, along with punctilious record keeping by the experimentalist [33,35]. The second issue; that of assigning an outcome to each experiment is more tractable, as there are already hundreds of millions of images which capture the output of the crystallisation experiment, due to the widespread adoption of imaging technology in crystallisation labs. What is missing is the reliable and widespread translation of the qualitative image data into quantitative data that could be used in downstream analyses. This process of assigning a value to an image (or to a visual inspection) of a crystallisation experiment is most often called *scoring*, and is the primary focus of this work. The third matter - the lack of tools for correlating the input to the output of an experiment is understandable given the limited amount of data available describing both the input and the output of most crystallisation trials. That is the failure to adequately solve issues one and two.

Analyses of images of crystallisation trials (a solution to the second issue) must fulfil two goals: most importantly, it has to aid in the identification of crystals that might be useful in diffraction experiments, or that might be used as the starting point for optimisation. The longer goal is to have a consistent set of annotations for data mining experiments which would improve the success rate of the current crystallisation process. Crystal formation happens rarely; although no hard numbers are available it is estimated that significantly less than 10% of outcomes are crystalline, which implies low tolerance for false negatives in crystal recognition. To complicate things further, there is no universally recognised set of classes into which images could be sorted, for either machine or human classification. Current scoring systems are generally one-dimensional: "crystal", "precipitate" and "clear". Images which have both crystals and precipitate would be generally annotated as "crystal", as that is the noteworthy outcome. Thus the current human annotations don't necessarily give a good description of what the drop image contains, but are more an indication of the most interesting component of the drop. The blurred boundaries of any crystal image classification system is highlighted by previous work which has shown less than 85% agreement for classification amongst human experts [48].

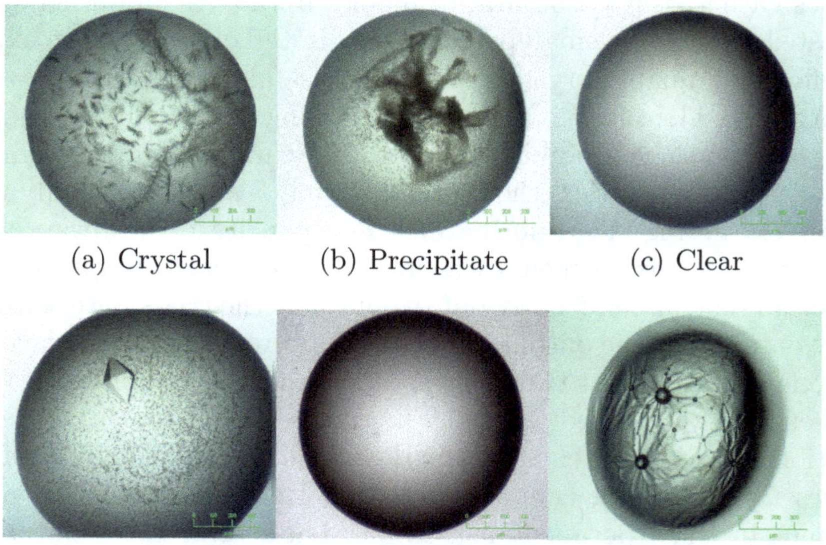

(a) Crystal (b) Precipitate (c) Clear

(d) Crystal + Precipitate (e) Plate features (f) skin

Fig. 2. Some example droplet images. Images a-c are clearly single class images (and labelled accordingly), however image d is an illustration of two classes (clear and precipitate) present in a single image. Images e-f are examples of difficult images. e shows a clear droplet where moulding features of the plastic substrate appear like crystals, f shows a droplet with a wrinkled protein skin covering the droplet.

This work presents an automated solution that applies this one-dimensional labelling scheme at scale in a fully distributed High Performance Computing (HPC) environment. We will give an overview of the data challenges, model development and parallelisation strategies used to ensure continuous and robust labelling of new droplet images in near real time.

2 Training and Testing Datasets

With its wealth of crystallisation data and access to world class machine learning engineers, C3 has pioneered the development of an automated classification pipeline, C4 (C3 Classifier), in an attempt to remedy the second problem outlined in Sect. 1, that of incomplete/noisy data about the output of crystallisation trials. To aid in the construction of the pipeline, C3 developed two high quality datasets to use for testing and training purposes, [36]. The images in these datasets were collected using a Rigaku Minstrel crystal imaging system which captured 5 megapixel images with a pixel width representing approximately 5 μm. The current imaging system is a Formulatrix RI1000 (www.formulatrix.com) which produces 5 megapixel images with a pixel width representing between 2 and 10 μm.

The first dataset, "Well Scored", is a collection of fourteen thousand images scored by a single expert into four classes as listed in Table 1. The second dataset, "One Year", is a collection of seventeen thousand images collected during the one year period between October 2014 and October 2015. As will be discussed in Sect. 4 the classification model currently in production scores images into the four classes used in the "Well Scored" dataset. Table 1 outlines the mapping from the original "One Year" class labels to the simpler four class system, as well as the mapping for an additional scoring system discussed in Sect. 4.

As will be discussed in Sect. 4 the classification model currently in production scores images into the four classes used in the "Well Scored" dataset. Table 1 outlines the mapping from the original "One Year" class labels to the simpler four class system, as well as the mapping for an additional scoring system discussed in Sect. 4.

In the experiments described in this work the "Well Scored" dataset was used as a completely separate held out test set. That is, we never used the "Well Scored" data for training. We trained all models on the "One Year" dataset and tested on the "Well Scored". This was primarily due to the empirical perception that the "One Year" dataset was more diverse than the "Well Scored" data, and thus provided a richer training set for the models. As we will discuss in the work that follows we found it particularly important to have a second, completely unseen, held out dataset. The generalisation of the model was of utmost importance and simply testing on a held out fraction of data was not enough to guarantee performance on similar data captured in a different crystallisation facility.

Finally Fig. 3 illustrates the distribution of images across the four classes described above. We can note a fairly similar distribution between the two different datasets, but it is also quite apparent the major over representation of the "crystal" and "precipitate" classes. This is due, in part, to the ambiguity of the definition for both the "clear" and "other" classes.

Table 1. Simplified four class mapping

Well scored	One year	DeepCrystal
Crystal	Crystals high	Alternate spectrum positive
	Crystals mid	Macro
	Crystals low	Micro
	Crystal	
	Crystalline	
	Salt crystals	
Precipitate	Bad precipitate	Precipitate amorphous
	Precipitate	Precipitate non-amorphous
	Good precipitate	
Clear	Clear	Clear
Other	Phase separation	Alternate spectrum negative
	Spherulites	Spherulites
	Clear with stuff	Dry
	Indeterminate	Skin
	Null experiment	Contaminants

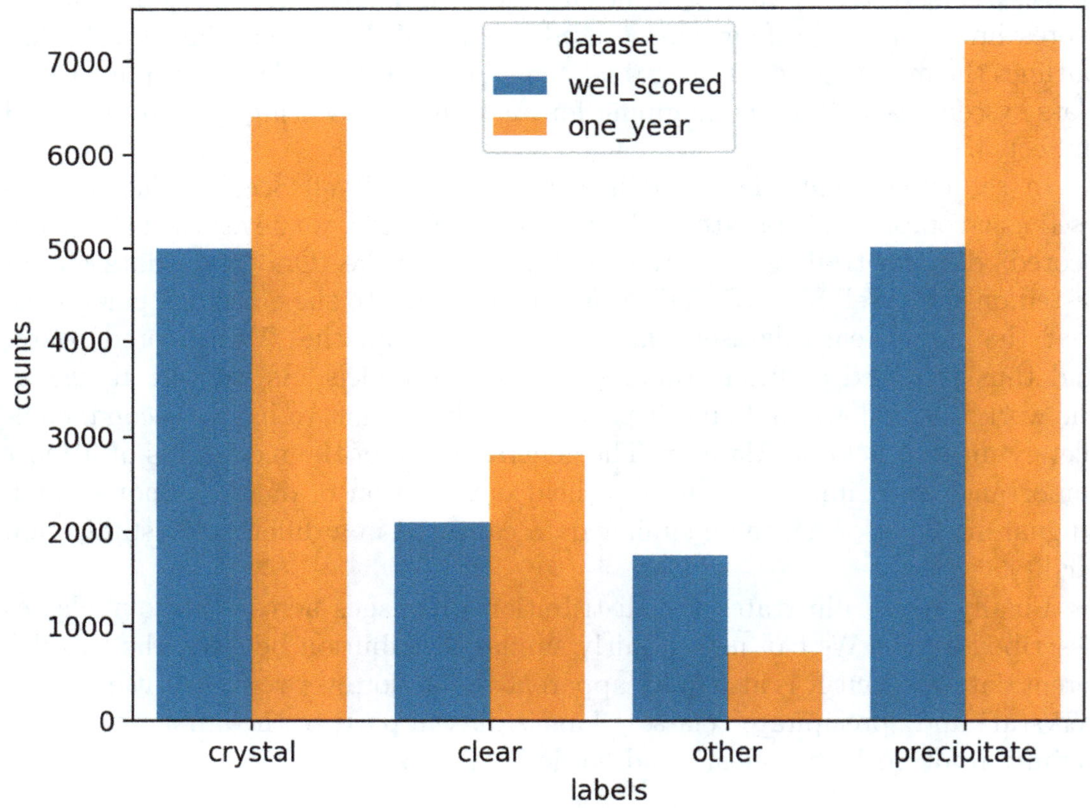

Fig. 3. Distribution of data points across the training (one_year) and validation (well_scored) datasets.

3 Early Attempts

Armed with an abundance of data and a targeted objective (generating accurate annotations for said data) the development of an automated classification pipeline began. This problem is important enough to have driven the development of several machine learning tools already, although none of these tools have been widely adopted, or even used outside of the laboratory in which they were initially developed. We began our work in the area by implementing three existing, externally developed, image classification tools in our own laboratory. See [46] for sample code. This was non-trivial, as none of the three applications we implemented (Besra [11], ALICE [48] and TexRank [34]) had been developed for anything but local use.

Besra was developed as a binary Support Vector Machine classifier [15], using the bag-of-visual-words [16] method to extract a feature vector. The visual vocabulary is computed from the training set by first extracting features (Speeded Up Robust Features [3]) and clustering them into a default 150 clusters using the bag of words k-means [3] clustering function in OpenCV [9]. This training is done on local images. By using Besra alone we obtained a $56.93 \pm 4.63\%$ accuracy when training a binary crystal/not crystal classifier and $63.77 \pm 5.0\%$ accuracy for the binary clear/not clear classifier, these results are summarised in Table 2.

ALICE is a pretrained classifier trained using $1024 \times 1024 \times 8$ bit grayscale bitmap images, corresponding to a pixel width of about 3 μm. It was built using Self-Organising Maps (SOMs) [25] and Learning Vector Quantisation (LVQ) [26] together with Bayesian probabilities [4]. Running ALICE on our test dataset gave an accuracy of $55.68 \pm 1.37\%$ accuracy when trained as a binary crystal/not crystal classifier and $75.90 \pm 2.49\%$ accuracy for the binary clear/not clear classifier, these results are summarised in Table 2. Although this was the poorest performing classifier its results were impressive given the fact that there was no training on local images.

Texrank is another pretrained algorithm, however, this tool was not developed as a classifier. Instead the algorithm was designed to rank a set of images according to their probability of containing a crystal. The ranking is performed by first extracting features by using a pretrained dictionary of textons [23], essentially a numerical descriptor of the textural features in a given image. This feature vector is then passed to a random forest classifier [43], the posterior probability obtained from the classifier is then used to rank droplets. The dataset used to train Texrank contained images with a resolution corresponding to a pixel width of about 4.5 μm. In our binary classification implementations we simply calculated a threshold on the "One Year" independently for both the crystal and clear classifiers. Running Texrank on our test dataset gave an accuracy of $75.03 \pm 0.96\%$ when trained as a binary crystal/not crystal classifier and $74.09 \pm 2.37\%$ accuracy for the binary clear/not clear classifier, these results are summarised in Table 2.

Finally, we amalgamated all three of these methods into a single binary classifier, *Combiner*, using a simple linear combination. We trained a single layer neural network on the "One Year" dataset, labelling the dataset for both crystal and clear classifications. Unsurprisingly the combined approach outperformed the individual techniques, although it never quite reached the level of human accuracy. Running Combiner on our test dataset gave an accuracy of 76.31 ± 2.78% when training a binary crystal/not crystal classifier and 85.12 ± 3.42% accuracy for the binary clear/not clear classifier, these results are summarised in Table 2.

Table 2. Classification accuracies for the binary crystal/not crystal and clear/not clear classifications models when applied to C3 data. Errors are given by the standard deviation over a 10-fold cross validation. The baseline value is generated by predicting each sample to be the majority class. Bold values represent the highest accuracy model for each classifier.

Classifier	Crystal	Clear
Baseline	63.87 %	84.87 %
Besra	56.93 ± 4.63%	63.77 ± 5.0%
ALICE	55.68 ± 1.37%	75.90 ± 2.49%
TexRank	75.03 ± 0.96%	74.09 ± 2.37%
Combiner	76.31 ± 2.78%	85.12 ± 3.42%
CNN	75.80 ± 2.54%	75.80 ± 2.10%
DeepCrystal	76.39 ± 1.00%	80.27 ± 1.01%
MARCO	**91.00 ± 5.00%**	**97.90 ± 5.00%**

During the development of these traditional hand crafted feature extraction approaches it was difficult to ignore the huge advances that were being made with deep learning, particularly in the image processing domains [20,27,39,42]. With this in mind we set out to develop a simple test network to evaluate the efficacy of the approach. Our initial experiments were built using tflearn [18] a Tensorflow [2] powered Python framework. The final network was a simple variant on the original AlexNet [27] architecture: four convolution layers [29] with ReLU activations [31] and max pooling followed by two dense layers with dropout for regularisation [40], the details of which are outlined in Table 3. The immense learning capacity of the network allowed it to outperform any of the traditional computer vision approaches and be on a comparable level to the combination of all methods. Although we were still below the level of human ability, this deep learning approach gave an accuracy of 75.80 ± 2.54% when trained as a binary crystal/not crystal classifier and 75.80 ± 2.10% accuracy for the binary clear/not clear classifier using our test dataset, these results are summarised (as CNN) in Table 2.

4 Deep Learning Solution

Motivated by the same advances in deep learning that excited us, the VC backed world of Silicon Valley has driven the development of a wealth of applications

Table 3. Preliminary convolutional neural network architecture.

Layer	Description
Input	$128 \times 128 \times 3$ RGB image
Convolution	3×3, 32 outputs, ReLU activation
Max pool	2×2
Convolution	3×3, 64 outputs, ReLU activation
Max pool	2×2
Convolution	3×3, 128 outputs, ReLU activation
Max pool	2×2
Convolution	3×3, 256 outputs, ReLU activation
Max pool	2×2
Dense	512 outputs, tanh activation
Dropout	dropout rate = 0.5
Dense	512 outputs, tanh activation
Dropout	dropout rate = 0.5
Dense	2 outputs

focused machine learning technology. Fortuitously one such application was in the area of machine learning for interpreting crystallisation images. This application was targeted at pharmaceutical and large biotech firms which use structural biology in their lead development pipeline. The recently acquired DeepCrystal (www.deepcrystal.com) had developed a 13-class droplet classification model based on Facebook's high performing convolutional architecture, ResNext [49]. The success of the DeepCrystal model was not so much due to the algorithm itself, which was an implementation of an existing tool, but lay in the diversity of their training data. Through their collaborations with both academic and private institutions (as well as a concentrated web-scraping effort) DeepCrystal was able to build a model with a (self reported) accuracy of 91%. An astounding result. In the spirit of collaboration C3 provided DeepCrystal with a small sample of competently scored images that were representative of those encountered at C3. In exchange DeepCrystal provided access to a closed, black-box implementation of their model, i.e. we were able to pass images in and get classifications out, however we were unable to modify or fine tune the model at all.

The closed nature of the model posed some challenges when trying to validate the claimed accuracy, and complicated comparisons to the other models implemented in C3. The comparison of results from the DeepCrystal model to the others implemented in C3 was stymied by the lack of accepted standards describing outcome classes of crystallisation experiments. We used the mapping shown in Table 1 to map the 13 classes of the DeepCrystal model to a simpler four class output for comparison. Two classes of the DeepCrystal model (the two Alternate Spectrum classes) are inappropriate for the visual light images that we used in our tests. Applying the class mapping we obtained an accuracy of $55.96 \pm 1.84\%$ for the four class scoring task. This poor performance is mostly likely due to the unclear mappings between DeepCrystal classes and C3 classes.

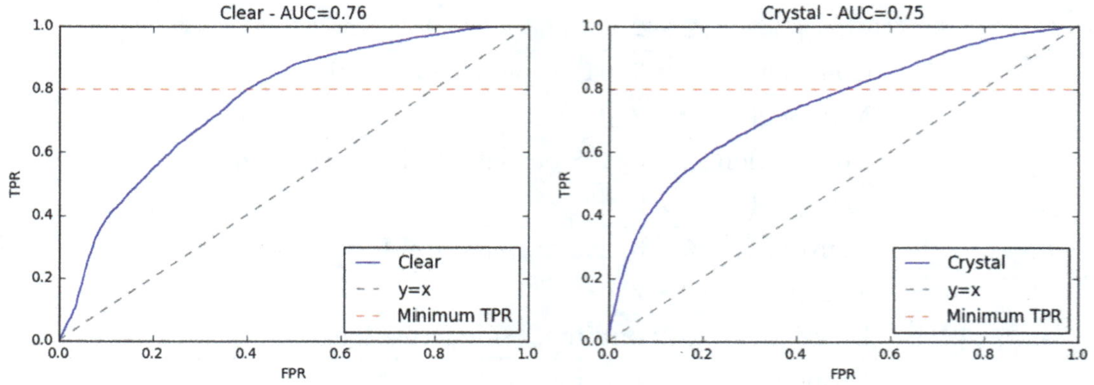

(a) Clear (b) Crystal

Fig. 4. Reciever Operator Characteristic curves for the binary DeepCrystal clear and crystal classifiers.

If we were able to modify the architecture we could simply have adjusted the output layer to match our classification system, and run a few epochs to fine tune the network, unfortunately that option was not possible. Instead the approach we took was to consider the output value for a single class and threshold that value to create a binary classifier. In the case of the crystal/not-crystal binary classifier we thresholded the "Macro" class, such that if "Macro" probability was above a certain value we would flag the presence of a crystal. Similarly for the clear/not-clear classifier we thresholded the "Clear" class. Using the holdout dataset we were able to optimise the threshold values by inspecting the behaviour of their corresponding ROC curves, shown in Figs. 4(a) and (b). The threshold values were found to be 0.4% and 4.3% for the "Clear" and "Macro" classes respectively. These values result in binary classification accuracies of $80.27 \pm 1.01\%$ for clear and $76.39 \pm 1.00\%$ for crystal. However, this system is still better than any of the other single tools, and performed similarly to Combiner, but had the advantage of being significantly simpler and faster than Combiner (in the sense that it was a single model). The ROC curves show far from ideal behaviour resulting in an appreciable false negative rate (FPR) even for low true positive rates (TPRs). In determining the optimum value for the threshold it was decided that an acceptable minimum TPR was 0.8. Users of the crystallisation centre are typically very intolerant of false negatives. Protein crystals are extremely hard to produce, and as such users *do not* want to miss any samples that may possibly contain a crystal. As a result users are more tolerant of false positives, that is, the inclusion of images with no crystals in the set containing crystals is an acceptable compromise in order to not miss any images that may contain crystals.

Around the time that DeepCrystal was being acquired and support for its improvement was lost the MAchine Recognition of Crystal Outcomes (MARCO) initiative was bearing fruit [12]. This collaborative effort between an international collection of academic institutions and pharmaceutical companies amassed a dataset of almost 500,000 images, which have been made publicly available, [14] and have been classified using the same four class system described in Sect. 2. The MARCO model uses the Inception-v3 architecture [41], has been trained using the open source MARCO dataset and has been open sourced itself [45], making it more flexible than our DeepCrystal implementation. Additionally MARCO reports some excellent results[1], producing accuracies of $97.90 \pm 5.00\%$ for clear and $91.00 \pm 5.00\%$ for crystal. Such results are far greater than any previously implemented approaches thus we now deploy the MARCO model as part of the image classifying pipeline discussed in Sect. 5.

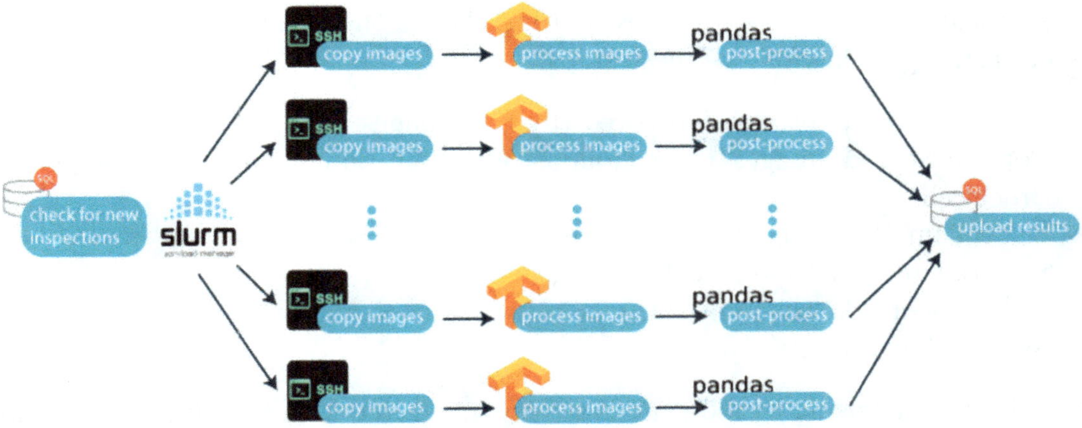

Fig. 5. Illustration of the C4 parallelisation scheme. Inspections of images are processed in parallel which are further classified in parallel on using GPU accelerated Tensorflow models.

5 Enabling Infrastructure

Previous sections have outlined the machine learning component of our solution: the models tested and how they are used. Here we will describe in more detail how the machine learning has been integrated into a fully autonomous end-to-end image classification pipeline, C3 Classifier (C4). This code is available at [47]. The two automated imagers in C3 (Formulatrix RI1000, www.formulatrix.com) produce JPG images of all droplets found in a single experimental plate – this is called an *inspection*; each inspection contains either 24 or 96 (or some multiple) images. Initially the images are stored locally on the imaging machine,

[1] The results reported here are those from [12], and thus have been produced using the MARCO dataset.

but are transferred almost immediately to a larger in-house cloud storage device (Bowen) for long term storage. Simultaneously the metadata for both the inspection and each image collected as part of the inspection is pushed into an Oracle database that is hosted in the same local cloud data centre. There are front-end applications which are available to the C3 users that allow them to inspect and classify images. Both the scores, and other associated information (scorer, score time) are captured in this same database. Scores generated by the machine learning tool are also stored in the database, the "scorer" field in the database is used to mark these as machine generated scores. Thus the database contains a record of all past and present images, noting which images have been classified, either manually by a human or automatically by our autonomous pipeline.

C4 is run from CSIRO's GPU cluster, Bracewell[2], which is composed of 114 Dell PowerEdge C4130 servers each with 4 NVIDIA Tesla P100s and dual Intel Xeon 14-core E5-2690 v4s connected on a FDR10 InfiniBand interconnect (a total of 456 GPUs, 228 Xeons; approximately 2.5 Pflops). This cluster is located in physically located about 600 Km from C3, at the Canberra Data Centre. Overall, the pipeline follows these steps:

- Check database for new, unscored (by C4) images
- Copy unscored images from cloud storage on Bowen to local storage on Bracewell
- Inspect images using the algorithms discussed in Sect. 4
- Save raw output to local cold storage
- Upload scores to the database
- Remove local image copies

C4 is written using Python and is tightly integrated with the Slurm Workload Manager. Some initial experiments were developed using the Luigi [8] workflow package for Python, but integration of Luigi with Slurm didn't fit the traditional High Performance Computing (HPC) model. A possible substitute is SciLuigi [28] which natively supports Slurm. The custom work flow employed by C4 has been modelled on Luigi: several distinct components, with checkpoints at the end of each component. The components of C4 are described in detail in the sections that follow and have been illustrated in Fig. 5.

5.1 Inspection Finder

C4 is set up to be run on an hourly basis, the initial execution is managed by a Cron job. Cron launches a single batch job which runs the Python script for inspecting the database for new inspections (via the Oracle ORM Python package). For each new un(auto)scored inspection a series of dependant batch jobs will be launched. This allows us to process all new inspections in parallel across the cluster. First the inspection classification script is queued. Then the post processing script is queued with the classification job listed as a dependency, so that it will not launch until the classification job has exited. Finally a data

[2] https://www.csiro.au/en/Research/Technology/Scientific-computing/Bracewell.

egress script is launched which has all of the previously submitted batch jobs (classification and post-processing) listed as dependencies. Only a single instance of this script is run and it will collate all the results and update the database with a single post so as to minimise the number of database connections. The post processing script also performs the clean up. All of these dependencies can be programatically determined, with their job IDs, from within Python. There are several Slurm Python wrappers, but we have made use of the PySlurm [37] implementation.

5.2 Inspection Classifier

Each individual classification job copies all the images in an inspection from Bowen cloud storage to node local Bracewell storage via `scp`. Specifically the copy is made using a combination of the Paramiko [19] and `scp` Python packages.

Once the image copy is complete the images are classified in parallel using the MARCO model discussed in Sect. 4. The MARCO model is an Inception-v3 architecture written using Tensorflow. The architecture and weights for the model can be obtained from [45]. As such the model can be called directly from within Python scripts and easily accelerated using the GPU. Images are currently processed in batches of 32. Probability distribution vectors returned from the MARCO model are saved into a temporary file as a means of checkpointing. Once the outputs had been successfully written to file we could remove the original inspection images and safely exit the program which would enable the corresponding post processing script to be executed when sufficient resources were available.

5.3 Post Processing

The post processing script takes the output probability distribution and identifies any interesting drops. Since replacing the DeepCrystal model with MARCO the post processing stage has become much simpler. First it reads in the temp file containing the probabilities for each image. Then it applies an argmax to the probability distribution, returning the most probably class prediction. These results are then saved in a new temp file, awaiting final processing.

5.4 Upload Results and Clean up

Once the all the inspections are processed the final data egress script will collate the results in all of the temp files and upload the interesting drops to the database in a single INSERT call, minimising the number of database connections the need to be made. The temp files are then removed, with the results probability files appended to a larger single file in long term storage.

5.5 Logging

With a fully autonomous pipeline running independently of human oversight, it can be quite tempting to simply assume it is running correctly. Software engineering best practices however, suggest that in these situations it is best to set up a logger, that is code which outputs information about the pipelines state at any given time. Using Python's logging package C4 has been able to build multiple loggers for each component of the pipeline. That is, each component has a regular logger printing to `stdout`, a debug logger printing to file as well as a custom logger that posts to a Slack channel in the project's team space. The Slack logger is the most important as experience has shown us how easy it is to forget to inspect log files. This custom logger will post selected updates to it's own channel, so as not to clutter the regular communication streams. The posts have also been formatted such that errors and progress updates are easily discernible, as well as the point of failure should an error occur. Future implementations of the logger will also send failure alerts via email, should Slack's current raging popularity diminish.

5.6 Cinder and Ashes

In an effort to improve the model on an ongoing basis we have begun collecting images that humans perceive MARCO has scored incorrectly. In a weekly Python script, Ashes, we identify any newly scored images where the human classification disagrees with the MARCO classification. These images are collected and saved for fine tuning in the future. However as discussed in Sect. 1 there is often disagreement among domain specialists as to what score to assign to images. Thus it is not enough to merely take the human score as the ground truth. To remedy this problem C3 has upgraded its image scoring app, Cinder [1] (Crystallographic Tinder), to allow for consensus scoring of badly scored images. That is to say, through the Cinder app users (generally crystallography experts) can score images that have been collected by Ashes. Once we have collected enough scores which are in agreement about a single image we can add that image to the data set for training, satisfied that its ground truth label is sufficiently accurate. This "citizen science" approach to data labelling has only begun recently and sufficient data has not yet been collected to begin the fine tuning process.

6 Deployment and Future Challenges

C4 has been in operation for over a year and its deployment has been well received. This has been most notably observed through a *reduction* in human scoring activity. C4 seamlessly processes up to twenty thousand images per day, casually fitting brief batch jobs into the typical HPC scheduler. A single inspection (~200 images) can be processed in under two minutes, with the majority of the processing time being consumed by data transport and database communication. While C4 is more than capable of keeping up with the continuously produced images, the ultimate goal of the C4 pipeline is to score the large backlog of over forty million images, enabling an understanding of the crystallisation landscape. While C4 has been designed with this goal in mind at present there are two limiting components: data ingress and data egress.

The server which manages the copying of data from storage to the compute is a low powered cloud machine. As such it cannot handle multiple connections over `ssh`. This has resulted in C4 limiting the number of simultaneous connections to the data server to ten, which ultimately stems the flow of data to the compute servers. We are currently investigating the root cause of the data flow problem, but it will most likely be solved by smarter scheduling around data handling. Similarly on the data egress front, the database does not accept a high number of simultaneous connections. This issue is currently handled by collating batches into a single upload, but this solution will not be acceptable nor stable enough to manage processing the backlog of data. One possible solution (for both ingress and egress) is to have some sort of data buffer that is periodically filled and emptied as required.

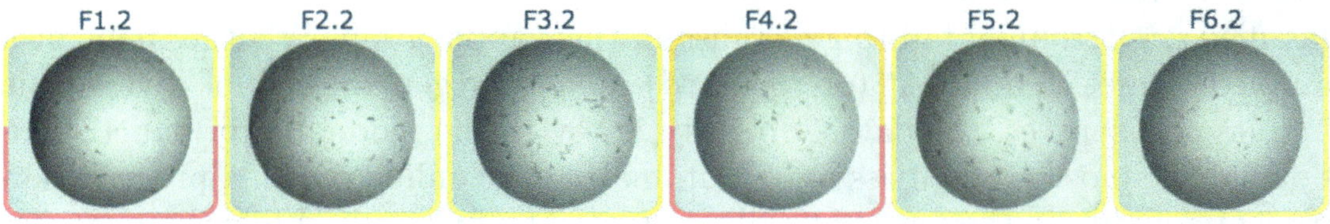

Fig. 6. An example visualisation from the See3 web inspection application available to C3 users. Typically users are shown an interface displaying thumbnails of their processed experiments. All scores are shown as border colours, The border starts at 9 o'clock and the colours are arranged so that user scores are shown first. An image with two scores will have two colours, with the upper colour being the human score, and the lower colour the machine score, an image with a single colour border has only been assigned a single score. (Color figure online)

With the droplet classifications stored in a database it is easy to integrate the findings into the existing C3 web application, See3. Figure 6 illustrates how the C4 classifications have been integrated into the See3 application. The yellow and orange colours on the upper border indicate that the user has assigned these images a crystal class (C3 uses multiple levels within the 4 broad categories in its classification system). The two samples F1.2 and F4.2 that have a pink lower border are images that have been flagged by C4 as containing crystals. The cases that have a single colour are images that have been scored only by the user, that is C4 has missed these images. You can see in this random sampling that C4 has missed quite a few instances of crystallisation.

The multiple shades for each class are an attempt at circumventing the class labelling issue discussed in Sect. 4. By refining the crystal (or other) class into more nuanced subclasses we are able to better capture the continuous nature of the crystallisation spectrum. In practice, there is not a discrete phase change from say, precipitate to crystal; there is a continuum between droplets containing only precipitate, droplets containing both precipitate and crystals and droplets containing only crystals; as such it can be difficult to define class boundaries. This partly explains the divergence of classification labels among domain specialists, with each expert identifying different features that are interesting to them. One potential approach to solving this problem may be to investigate the use of unsupervised learning methods. Given that C3 has a wealth of unlabelled diverse data we could use this to train an unsupervised feature extractor, something like a convolutional autoencoder [5]. The features learned by the autoencoder could then be used by a clustering algorithm, perhaps t-Stochastic Neighbourhood Embedding [44], to find local groups of visually similar images. If obviously distinct classes cannot be differentiated perhaps at least some intuition as to how the droplet classes can be arranged together. Additionally, the labelled and unlabelled datasets could be combined in a semi-supervised scheme similar to [6,21,22] or [24].

One of the fundamental lessons we have learned is that the diversity of the data set is of critical importance. We have experienced a number of times that models trained on datasets that do not accurately represent the data to be classified post training fail to generalise in their application. Whether it be over sampled classes, redundant (or repeated) images or general lack of diversity in samples and sources, the dataset quality is key to the model performance. This is one of the most pressing issues in automating the online training process; how to ensure quality in the automatically extracted training set. While there is some work that suggests deep neural networks are robust to noise in the training data [38], when we are trying to fine tune a network it will be quality, well classified images from the boundaries of the class domains that will ensure a robust and reliable model moving forward.

7 Conclusions

C3 has developed and deployed a reliable and robust autonomous classification system for protein crystallisation images. The system has been deployed in a production system delivering almost real time results through the massive parallelisation of image processing. The pipeline has received qualitatively good feedback on its performance, although it is clear that further development is required. With the ability to compare human and machine scores C3 is now seeking to develop an online training technique by mining hard-to-classify images.

References

1. Cinder "crystallographic tinder". https://research.csiro.au/crystal/user-guide/c3-cinder/. Accessed 02 Jan 2019
2. Abadi, M., et al.: TensorFlow: large-scale machine learning on heterogeneous distributed systems March 2016. http://arxiv.org/abs/1603.04467

3. Bay, H., Tuytelaars, T., Van Gool, L.: SURF: speeded up robust features. In: Leonardis, A., Bischof, H., Pinz, A. (eds.) ECCV 2006. LNCS, vol. 3951, pp. 404–417. Springer, Heidelberg (2006). https://doi.org/10.1007/11744023_32
4. Bayes, F.R.S.: An Essay towards Solving a Problem in the Doctrine of Chances. Philos. Trans. R. Soc. Lond. **53**(0), 370–418 (1763). https://doi.org/10.1098/rstl.1763.0053
5. Bengio, Y.: Learning deep architectures for AI. Found. Trends® Mach. Learn. **2**(1), 1–127 (2009). https://doi.org/10.1561/2200000006. www.nowpublishers.com/article/Details/MAL-006
6. Bengio, Y., Lamblin, P., Popovici, D., Larochelle, H.: Greedy layer-wise training of deep networks. In: Schölkopf, B., Platt, J.C., Hoffman, T. (eds.) Advances in Neural Information Processing Systems 19, pp. 153–160. MIT Press (2007). http://papers.nips.cc/paper/3048-greedy-layer-wise-training-of-deep-networks.pdf
7. Rupp, B.: Garland Science - Book: Biomolecular Crystallography + 1. Garland Science, 1st edn. (2009). http://www.garlandscience.com/product/isbn/9780815340812
8. Bernhardsson, E., Freider, E., Rouhani, A.: Luigi (2012). https://github.com/spotify/luigi
9. Bradski, G.: The OpenCV library. Dr. Dobb's J. Soft. Tools (2000)
10. Brändén, C.I., Tooze, J.: Introduction to Protein Structure. Garland Pub, Spokane (1999)
11. Bruno, A.E.: Besra (2015). https://doi.org/10.5281/zenodo.60970, https://www.researchgate.net/publication/309319298_Besra
12. Bruno, A.E., et al.: Classification of crystallization outcomes using deep convolutional neural networks. PLoS One **13**(6) (2018). https://doi.org/10.1371/journal.pone.0198883
13. Carter, C.W., Carter, C.W.: Protein crystallization using incomplete factorial experiments. J. Biol. Chem. **254**(23), 12219–12223 (1979). www.jbc.org/cgi/content/short/254/23/12219
14. Charbonneau, P.: Machine recognition of crystal outcomes (2018)
15. Cortes, C., Vapnik, V.: Support-vector networks. Mach. Learn. **20**(3), 273–297 (1995). https://doi.org/10.1007/BF00994018
16. Csurka, G., Csurka, G., Dance, C.R., Fan, L., Willamowski, J., Bray, C.: Visual categorization with bags of keypoints. In: Workshop on Statistical Learning in Computer Vision, ECCV, pp. 1–22 (2004). http://citeseerx.ist.psu.edu/viewdoc/summary?doi=10.1.1.72.604
17. Cudney, R., Patel, S., Weisgraber, K., Newhouse, Y., McPherson, A.: Screening and optimization strategies for macromolecular crystal growth. Acta Crystallogr. Sect. D Biol. Crystallogr. **50**(4), 414–423 (1994). https://doi.org/10.1107/S0907444994002660. http://www.ncbi.nlm.nih.gov/pubmed/15299395
18. Damien, A., et al.: TFLearn (2016)
19. Forcier, J.: Paramiko (2017)
20. He, K., Zhang, X., Ren, S., Sun, J.: Deep residual learning for image recognition (2015). http://arxiv.org/abs/1512.03385
21. Hinton, G.E., Salakhutdinov, R.R.: Reducing the dimensionality of data with neural networks. Science **313**(5786), 504–507 (2006). https://doi.org/10.1126/science.1127647. www.science.sciencemag.org/content/313/5786/504
22. Jarrett, K., Kavukcuoglu, K., Ranzato, M., LeCun, Y.: What is the best multi-stage architecture for object recognition? In: 2009 IEEE 12th International Conference on Computer Vision, pp. 2146–2153, September 2009. https://doi.org/10.1109/ICCV.2009.5459469

23. Julesz, B.: Textons, the elements of texture perception and their interactions. Nature **290**(5802), 91–97 (1981). https://doi.org/10.1038/290091a0. www.nature.com/doifinder/10.1038/290091a0
24. Kavukcuoglu, K., Sermanet, P., lan Boureau, Y., Gregor, K., Mathieu, M., Cun, Y.L.: Learning convolutional feature hierarchies for visual recognition. In: Lafferty, J.D., Williams, C.K.I., Shawe-Taylor, J., Zemel, R.S., Culotta, A. (eds.) Advances in Neural Information Processing Systems, vol. 23, pp. 1090–1098. Curran Associates, Inc. (2010). http://papers.nips.cc/paper/4133-learning-convolutional-feature-hierarchies-for-visual-recognition.pdf
25. Kohonen, T.: Self-organized formation of topologically correct feature maps. Biol. Cybern. **43**(1), 59–69 (1982). https://doi.org/10.1007/BF00337288
26. Kohonen, T.: Learning Vector Quantization. Springer, Heidelberg (2001). https://doi.org/10.1007/978-3-642-56927-2_6
27. Krizhevsky, A., Sutskever, I., Hinton, G.E.: ImageNet classification with deep convolutional neural networks. In: Advances in Neural Information Processing Systems, vol. 25, pp. 1097–1105 (2012)
28. Lampa, S., Alvarsson, J., Spjuth, O.: Towards agile large-scale predictive modelling in drug discovery with flow-based programming design principles. J. Cheminformatics **8**(1), 67 (2016). https://doi.org/10.1186/s13321-016-0179-6
29. Lecun, Y., Bottou, L., Bengio, Y., Haffner, P.: Gradient-based learning applied to document recognition. Proc. IEEE **86**(11), 2278–2324 (1998). https://doi.org/10.1109/5.726791
30. Luft, J.R., Newman, J., Snell, E.H.: Crystallization screening the influence of history on current practice. Acta Crystallogr. Sect. F Struct. Biol. Commun **70**(7), 835–53 (2014). https://doi.org/10.1107/S2053230X1401262X. www.ncbi.nlm.nih.gov/pubmed/25005076
31. Nair, V., Hinton, G.E.: Rectified linear units improve restricted Boltzmann machines. In: Proceedings of the 27th International Conference on Machine Learning, vol. 3, pp. 807–814, Haifa, Israel (2010). https://doi.org/10.1.1.165.6419. http://www.cs.toronto.edu/fritz/absps/reluICML.pdf
32. Newman, J., et al.: On the need for an international effort to capture, share and use crystallization screening data. Acta Crystallogr. Sect. F Struct. Biol. Crystallization Commun. **68**(3), 253–258 (2012). https://doi.org/10.1107/S1744309112002618. www.ncbi.nlm.nih.gov/pubmed/22442216
33. Newman, J., Peat, T.S., Savage, G.P.: What's in a name? Moving towards a limited vocabulary for macromolecular crystallisation. Aust. J. Chem. **67**(12), 1813 (2014). https://doi.org/10.1071/CH14199. www.publish.csiro.au/?paper=CH14199
34. Ng, J.T., Dekker, C., Kroemer, M., Osborne, M., von Delft, F.: Using textons to rank crystallization droplets by the likely presence of crystals. Acta crystallogr. Sect. D, Biol. crystallogr. **70**(10), 2702–2718 (2014). https://doi.org/10.1107/S1399004714017581. www.ncbi.nlm.nih.gov/pubmed/25286854
35. Ng, J.T., Dekker, C., Reardon, P., von Delft, F.: Lessons from ten years of crystallization experiments at the SGC. Acta Crystallogr. Sect. D Struct. Biol. **72**(2), 224–35 (2016). https://doi.org/10.1107/S2059798315024687. www.ncbi.nlm.nih.gov/pubmed/26894670
36. Ratcliffe, D., Carroll, T., Watkins, C., Newman, J.: CSIRO data access portal - crystallisation images from C3 (2016). https://data.csiro.au/dap/landingpage?pid=csiro:20158&v=3&d=true
37. Roberts, M., Torres, G.: PySlurm (2017). https://pyslurm.github.io/
38. Rolnick, D., Veit, A., Belongie, S., Shavit, N.: Deep learning is robust to massive label noise, May 2017. http://arxiv.org/abs/1705.10694

39. Simonyan, K., Zisserman, A.: Very deep convolutional networks for large-scale image recognition, September 2014. http://arxiv.org/abs/1409.1556
40. Srivastava, N., Hinton, G., Krizhevsky, A., Sutskever, I., Salakhutdinov, R.: Dropout: a simple way to prevent neural networks from overfitting. J. Mach. Learn. Res. **15**, 1929–1958 (2014). https://doi.org/10.1214/12-AOS1000
41. Szegedy, C., Vanhoucke, V., Ioffe, S., Shlens, J., Wojna, Z.: Rethinking the inception architecture for computer vision. In: 2016 IEEE Conference on Computer Vision and Pattern Recognition (CVPR), pp. 2818–2826, June 2016. https://doi.org/10.1109/CVPR.2016.308
42. Szegedy, C., et al.: Going deeper with convolutions, September 2014. http://arxiv.org/abs/1409.4842
43. Ho, T.K.: The random subspace method for constructing decision forests. IEEE Trans. Pattern Anal. Mach. Intell. **20**(8), 832–844 (1998). https://doi.org/10.1109/34.709601
44. Van Der Maaten, L., Hinton, G.: Visualizing Data using t-SNE. J. Mach. Learn. Res. **9**, 2579–2605 (2008). www.jmlr.org/papers/volume9/vandermaaten08a/vandermaaten08a.pdf
45. Vanhoucke, V.: Automating the evaluation of crystallization experiments. https://github.com/tensorflow/models/tree/master/research/marco (2018)
46. Watkins, C.J.: C3 Computer vision algorithms (2017). https://data.csiro.au/dap/landingpage?pid=csiro:29414
47. Watkins, C.J.: C4–C3 Classification pipeline (2018). https://data.csiro.au/dap/landingpage?pid=csiro:29413
48. Watts, D., Cowtan, K., Wilson, J.: IUCr: automated classification of crystallization experiments using wavelets and statistical texture characterization techniques. J. Appl. Crystallogr. **41**(1), 8–17 (2008). https://doi.org/10.1107/S0021889807049308
49. Xie, S., Girshick, R., Dollár, P., Tu, Z., He, K.: Aggregated residual transformations for deep neural networks, November 2016. http://arxiv.org/abs/1611.05431

A Cache-Based Data Movement Infrastructure for On-demand Scientific Cloud Computing

David Abramson[1(✉)], Jake Carroll[1], Chao Jin[1], Michael Mallon[1], Zane van Iperen[1], Hoang Nguyen[1], Allan McRae[1], and Liang Ming[2]

[1] The University of Queensland, St Lucia, QLD 4072, Australia
{david.abramson, jake.carroll, c.jin, m.mallon, z.vaniperen, h.nguyen30, a.mcrae}@uq.edu.au
[2] Huawei Technologies Co., Ltd., Shenzhen, China
l.ming@huawei.com

Abstract. As cloud computing has become the de facto standard for big data processing, there is interest in using a multi-cloud environment that combines public cloud resources with private on-premise infrastructure. However, by decentralizing the infrastructure, a uniform storage solution is required to provide data movement between different clouds to assist on-demand computing. This paper presents a solution based on our earlier work, the MeDiCI (Metropolitan Data Caching Infrastructure) architecture. Specially, we extend MeDiCI to simplify the movement of data between different clouds and a centralized storage site. It uses a hierarchical caching system and supports most popular infrastructure-as-a-service (IaaS) interfaces, including Amazon AWS and OpenStack. As a result, our system allows the existing parallel data intensive application to be offloaded into IaaS clouds directly. The solution is illustrated using a large bioinformatics application, a Genome Wide Association Study (GWAS), with Amazons AWS, HUAWEI Cloud, and a private centralized storage system. The system is evaluated on Amazon AWS and the Australian national cloud.

Keywords: Cloud · Big data · Caching · Data migration

1 Introduction

Presently, many big data workloads operate across isolated data stores that are distributed geographically and manipulated by different clouds. For example, the typical scientific data processing pipeline [26, 40] consists of multiple stages that are frequently conducted by different research organizations with varied computing demands. Accordingly, accelerating data analysis for each stage may require computing facilities that are located in different clouds. Between different stages of the geographical data pipeline, moving a large amount of data across clouds is common [5, 37]. This type of multi-cloud environment can consist of resources from multiple public cloud vendors, such as Amazon AWS [1] and Microsoft Azure [29], and private data centers. Multi-cloud is used for many reasons, such as best-fit performance, increased fault tolerance, lower cost, reduced risk of vendor lock-in, privacy, security, and legal restrictions.

D. Abramson and B. R. de Supinski (Eds.): SCFA 2019, LNCS 11416, pp. 38–56, 2019.
https://doi.org/10.1007/978-3-030-18645-6_3

Different from hybrid-cloud, however, data silos in multi-cloud are isolated by varied storage mechanisms of different vendors. This complicates applying on-demand computing for scientific research across clouds. Although computation offloading into clouds is standardized with virtual machines, a typical data processing pipeline faces multiple challenges in moving data between clouds. First, a uniform way of managing and moving data is required across different clouds. Second, the network connections for inter-clouds and intra-cloud are typically different in terms of bandwidth and security. Moving a large amount of data between centers must utilize critical resources such as network bandwidth efficiently, and resolve the difficulties of latency and stability issues associated with long-haul networks. Third, users have to maintain the consistency of duplicated copies between silos with different storage mechanisms. Fourth, data migration between the stages of a pipeline needs to cooperate efficiently with computing tasks scheduling.

In this work, we propose a hierarchical global caching architecture across geographical data centers of different clouds. Such a system supports automatic data migration to cooperate on-demand Cloud computing. It unifies distant data silos using a file system interface (POSIX) and provides a global namespace across different clouds, while hiding the technical difficulties from users. Data movement between distant data centers is made automatic using caching. Our high performance design supports massive data migration required by scientific computing. Our previous work, called MeDiCI [10], has been shown to work well in an environment consisting of private data centers dispersed across the metropolitan area. In this paper, we extend MeDiCI into the multi-cloud environment that consists of most popular infrastructure-as-a-service (IaaS) cloud platforms, including Amazon AWS and OpenStack-based public clouds, and Australian data centers of NeCTAR (The National eResearch Collaboration Tools and Resources). Existing parallel data intensive applications are allowed to run in the virtualized resources directly without significant modifications.

This paper mainly discusses the following innovations:

- A global caching architecture that moves data across clouds in accordance with on-demand compute and storage resource acquirement;
- A demonstration of the proposed architecture using parallel file system components;
- A platform independent mechanism that manages the system across different IaaS clouds, including Amazon AWS and OpenStack-based clouds;
- Demonstrating our solution using a Genome Wide Association Study with resources from Amazon Sydney and a centralized storage site in Brisbane.

The rest of the paper is organized as follows. Section 2 provides an overview of related work and our motivation. Section 3 introduces our proposed global caching architecture. Sections 4 describe the realization of our storage architecture. Section 5 provides a detailed case study in Amazon EC2 and HUAWEI Cloud with according performance evaluation. Our conclusions follow in Sect. 6.

2 Background

Massive data analysis in the scientific domain [26, 30] needs to process data that is generated from a rich variety of sources, including scientific simulations, instruments, sensors, and Internet services. Many data intensive applications are embarrassingly parallel and can be accelerated using the high throughput model of cloud computing. Therefore, complementing private data centers with on-demand resources drawn from multiple (public) clouds is frequently used to tolerate compute demand increases. However, offloading computation into clouds not only requires acquiring compute resources dynamically, but also moving target data into the allocated virtual machines. Most existing storage solutions are not designed for a multi-cloud environment. In particular, they often require users to move data between processing steps of a geographical data processing pipeline explicitly. In addition, many existing methods do not directly support parallel IO to improve the performance of scalable data analysis. This section reviews the existing methods and motivates our solution.

"Data diffusion" [19, 20], which can acquire compute and storage resources dynamically, replicate data in response to demand, and schedule computations close to data, has been proposed for Grid computing. In the cloud era, the idea has been extended to scientific workflows that schedule compute tasks [40] and move required data across the global deployment of cloud centers. Both data diffusion and cloud workflows rely on a centralized site that provides data-aware compute tasks scheduling and supports an index service to locate data sets dispersed globally. In contrast, our model suits a loosely coupled working environment in which no central service of task scheduling and data index is required. Actually, each department controls its own compute resources and the collaboration between departments relies on shared data sets that are stored in a central site for long-term use. Our previous solution, MeDiCI [10], works well on dedicated resources. In this paper, we extend MeDiCI to a multi-cloud environment with dynamic resources and varied storage mechanisms.

A substantial portion of our work needs to move data across different clouds efficiently. Cloud storage systems, such as Amazon S3 [1] and Microsoft Azure [29], provide specific methods to exchange data across centers within a single cloud, and mechanisms are available to assist users to migrate data into cloud data centers. For instance, the Microsoft Azure Data Factory and the AWS Data Pipeline support data-driven workflows in the cloud to orchestrate and to automate data movement and data transformation. These cloud specific solutions mainly handle data in the format of cloud objects and database. Some other workflow projects combine cloud storage, such Amazon S3, with local parallel file systems to provide a hybrid solution. For example, a staging site [25] is introduced for Pegasus Workflow Management System to convert between data objects and files and supports both Cloud and Grid facilities. In comparison, some cloud backup solutions, such as Dropbox [9], NextCloud [33], and SPANStore [44], provide seamless data access to different clouds. However, most of these cloud storage solutions do not directly support parallel IO that is favored by embarrassing parallel data intensive applications.

Recent projects support directly transferring files between sites to improve overall system efficiency [38]. For example, OverFlow [37, 39] provides a uniform storage management system for multi-site workflows that utilize the local disks associated with virtual machine instances. It extends replication service to handle data transfer for inter-site and intra-site traffic using different protocols and mechanisms. This type of customized storage solution is designed to cooperate with the target workflow scheduler using a set of special storage APIs.

The distributed file system provides a general storage interface widely used by almost all parallel applications. How to support a distributed file system in the global environment has been investigated extensively [6, 12, 14, 22, 23, 27, 32, 41]. Typically, the tradeoff between performance, consistency, and data availability must be compromised appropriately to address the targeted data access patterns. Most general distributed file systems designed for the global environment focus on consistency at the expense of performance. The Andrew File System (AFS) [24] federates a set of trusted servers to provide a consistent and location independent global namespace to all of its clients. The AFS caching mechanism allows accessing files over a network as if they were on a local disk. OpenAFS [34] is an open source software project implementing the AFS protocol. Exposing clustered file systems, such as GPFS and Lustre, to personal computers using OpenAFS has been investigated [18]. Frequently, AFS caching suffers from performance issues due to overrated consistency and a complex caching protocol [28]. Overall, AFS was not designed to support large-scale data movement required by on-demand scientific computing. The similar idea of using a global caching system to transfer data in a wide area was also investigated by Content Delivery Networks (CDN) [12]. CDN caches site content at the edge of the Internet, close to end users, in order to improves website performance. In comparison, BAD-FS [21] and Panache [31] improve data movement onto remote computing clusters distributed across the wide area, in order to assist dynamic computing resource allocation. BAD-FS supports batch-aware data transfer between remote clusters in a wide area by exposing the control of storage policies such as caching, replication, and consistency and enabling explicit and workload-specific management. Panache is a scalable, high-performance, clustered file system cache that supports wide area file access while tolerating WAN (Wide Area Network) latencies. It transfers remote files in parallel using the NFS protocol, instead of other batch mode data movement solutions, such as GridFTP [42] and GlobusOnline [7]. Panache maintains the consistency of both meta-data and files.

Our previous work, MeDiCI [10], builds on AFM [17], which is a commercial version of Panache. MeDiCI constructs a hierarchical caching system using AFM and parallel file systems. MeDiCI exploits temporal and spatial locality to move data on demand in an automated manner across our private data centers that spans the metropolitan area. With this paper, we extend MeDiCI to (1) unify the varied storage mechanisms across clouds using the POSIX interface; and (2) provide a data movement infrastructure to assist on-demand scientific computing in a multi-cloud environment.

3 Design

A geographical data processing pipeline may consist of multiple stages and each stage could be executed in different data centers that have appropriate computing facilities. Each stage needs to process both local data and remote files, which require moving data from a remote center to the local site. After each stage is finished, the migrated data can be deleted according to the specific request, while the generated output may be collected. Frequently, a central storage site keeps long-term use data for pipelines. The common data access patterns of these pipelines include data dissemination, collection, and aggregation [37]. In addition, concurrent data write operations across different phases are very rare.

Our global caching infrastructure aims to support this type of data pipeline that are performed using compute resources allocated dynamically in IaaS clouds. Our system provides a POSIX interface and supports parallel IO to the data intensive applications running in a virtual cluster. With this storage infrastructure, applications do not have to be modified and can be offloaded into clouds directly.

In particular, this global caching architecture accommodates on-demand data movement across different clouds to meet the following requirements: (1) a unified storage solution for multi-cloud; (2) automatic on-demand data movement to fetch data from a remote site; (3) facilitating parallel IO for high performance computing directly; (4) supporting data access patterns commonly used; and (5) efficiently utilizing the network bandwidth to transfer a large amount of data over distant centers.

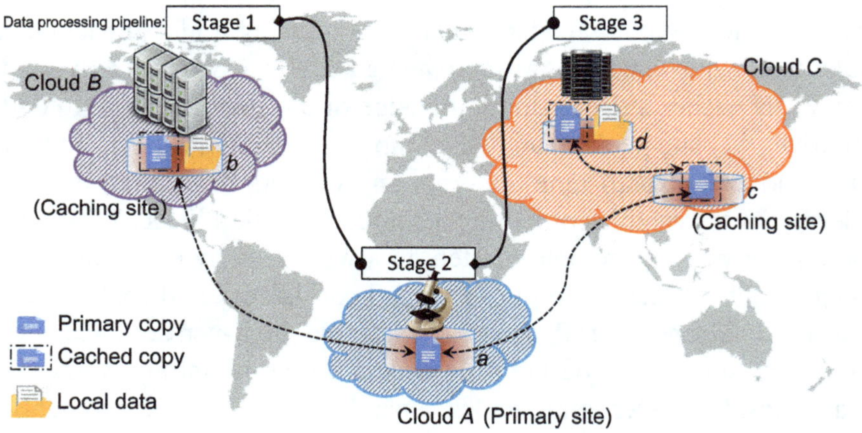

Fig. 1. The hierarchical caching architecture across different clouds.

Our design principle builds on the following key factors.

A global namespace with a POSIX interface: most high performance computing applications rely on a traditional file interface, instead of the cloud objects. Exposing a file interface can save the extra effort of converting between files and objects and it works with many existing scientific applications seamlessly. Furthermore, the global namespace across different clouds allow multiple research organizations share the same set of data without concerning its exact location.

A hierarchical caching architecture: the caching architecture aims to migrate remote data to locate sites in an automated manner without user's direct involvement. In addition, it takes advantage of data location to save unnecessary data transfer.

Data consistency model for the target data access patterns: appropriate data consistency model is critical for the global performance and latency perceived by applications. Our consistency model supports common data access patterns, such as data dissemination and data collections.

Network optimization for distant connections: our system should support optimized global network path with multiple hops, and improve the usage of limited network bandwidth.

The expense of acquiring virtual clusters is out of the scope of this paper. In particular, we expect that users should be aware of whether the advantage of using a remote virtual cluster offsets the network costs caused by significant inter-site data transfer.

3.1 Hierarchical Global Caching Architecture

Many distributed storage systems use caching to improve performance by reducing remote data access. Different from other work, our global caching architecture uses caching to automate data migration across distant centers. The proposed caching model assumes that each data set in the global domain has a primary site and can be cached across multiple remote centers using a hierarchical structure, as exemplified in Fig. 1, in which the primary site is the central storage center for keeping long-term use data. Each data set has a primary copy maintained by its primary site and multiple cached copies maintained by caching sites. The primary copy and cached copies form a tree structure, in which the primary copy is the root. As illustrated in Fig. 1, the primary copy is maintained by Cloud *A* on site *a* and it is cached in Cloud *B* and *C* respectively. In Cloud *C*, the data is cached on two sites, *c* and *d*.

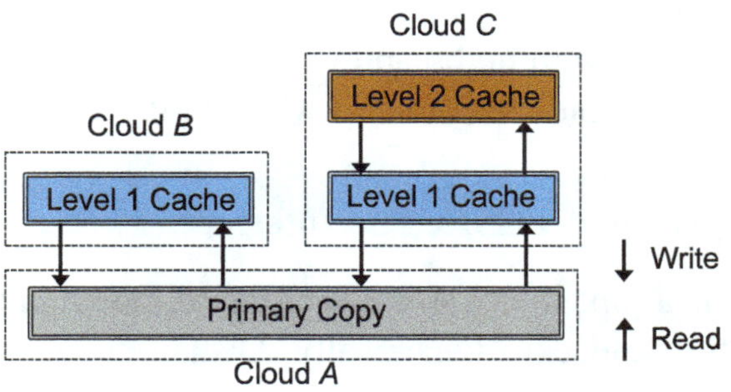

Fig. 2. Data movement path.

Each file in this system can have multiple replicas across data centers that are identified using the same logical name. Within a single data site, a replica is controlled by the local storage solution, typically a parallel file system, which may use data duplication to improve performance. All the copies in a single center are taken as a single logical copy. Across data centers, duplications of logical replicas and their consistency are managed by the global caching architecture. Users are not aware of the exact location for each data set. However, data is actually moved between geographically distributed caching sites according to data processing requirements, in order to lower the latency to frequently accessed data. The migrated data set typically stays locally for the term of use, instead of permanently. The basic data migration operations are supported: (1) fetching remote files to the local site; and (2) sending local updates to a remote site. These two basic operations can be composed to support the common data access patterns, such as data dissemination, data aggregation and data collection.

Data movement is triggered on-demand, although pre-fetch can be used to hide the latency according to the exact data access patterns. Cache capacity on each site is configurable, and an appropriate data eviction algorithm is used to maximize data reuse. In the hierarchical caching architecture, data movement only occurs between neighbor layers. Figure 2 illustrates the data movement path for the caching architecture of Fig. 1. The top tier caching serves any requested data from the next layer of cache in line. When a cache miss occurs, the request will be forwarded to the next tier of the hierarchical cache, until the primary site is reached. Typically, a read operation moves data from the primary site to the targeted caching site layer by layer, while writes are committed in a reverse order to the primary site.

The hierarchical structure enables moving data through intermediate sites. This layered caching architecture can be adopted in two scenarios: (1) improving the usage of local data copies while decreasing remote data access; and (2) data movement adapted to the global topology of network connections. The exact path to transfer data from the source site to the destination center should be optimized, because the direct network path between two sites may not be the fastest one. In particular, all of the available global network paths should be examined to take advantage path and file splitting [15]. Sometime, adding an intermediate hop between source and destination sites performs better than the direct link. This feature can be achieved by using the hierarchical caching structure naturally. Transferring data via an intermediate site only need to add the cached directory for the target data set, as described in Sect. 3.2. For example, in Fig. 1, assume site a has poor direct network connection with site d, but site c connects both a and d with high bandwidth network. Therefore, site a can move data to d using site c as an intermediate hop with the layered caching structure.

3.2 Global Namespace and POSIX File Interface

With a geographical data pipeline, we envisage that different cloud facilities can take part in the collaboration and exit dynamically. Distant collaborative sites should be loosely coupled. Accordingly, we need a flexible method to construct the storage system across different clouds. In order to allow data to be exchanged transparently across different clouds, a consistent and uniform namespace needs to span a set of distant centers. In addition, different from many other systems, our caching architecture does not maintain a global membership service that monitors whether a data center is online or offline. This saves the overhead of keeping the location of each piece of data in multi-cloud.

The global namespace is provided using the POSIX file interface, and is constructed by linking the remote data set to a directory in the local file system. In other words, a local directory is specified to hold the cache for the remote data set. Multiple remote data sets, which may originate from different data centers, can be stored in different directories on the same site. Therefore, a POSIX file interface unifies storage access for both local and remote data. The cached remote directory has no difference from other local directories, except its files are copied remotely whenever necessary.

3.3 Storage Organization of a Caching Site

In each site, a local parallel file system is used to maintain both cached remote data and local files accessed by the parallel applications running in the virtual cluster. The local parallel file system can be installed on dedicated storage resources to work as a shared storage service, or located on storage devices associated with the same set of compute resources allocated for the data analysis job. The first option maintains cached data for long-term usage, while the second option suits short-term data maintenance, because data storage is normally discarded after computing is finished. The storage media used in each site can be multi-tiered, using varied storage devices such as SSD and hard disk drives. How to organize the storage media to host the parallel file system is out of the scope of this paper.

3.4 Data Consistency

To accommodate common data access patterns used in typical data analysis pipelines, we adopt a consistency model to prioritize data access performance while providing acceptable consistency. In particular, data consistency within a single site is guaranteed by the local parallel file system. Across distant sites, a weak consistency semantic is supported across shared files and a lazy synchronization protocol is adopted to save unnecessary remote data movement. Remote files are copied only when they are accessed. However, a prefetching policy can be specified to hide the latency of moving data, such as copying neighbor files when one file in a directory is accessed. The validity of cached files is actively maintained by each caching site. The validity is verified both periodically and when directories and files are accessed. In addition, users can select an appropriate policy for output files, such as write-through or write-back, to optimize performance and resilience.

The updates on large files are synchronized using a lazy consistency policy, while meta-data is synchronized using a prompt policy. Assuming each caching site verifies its validation every f seconds, for an n level caching hierarchy, the protocol guarantees that the whole system reaches consistency on updated meta-data within $2n \cdot f$ seconds. This consistency model supports data dissemination and collections very well across distant sites on huge files, according to our experience.

3.5 Component Interaction

Figure 3 illustrates the major components that realize the global caching architecture across distant sites. A POSIX file interface spans different clouds to provide a uniform storage access interface. In each site, different native parallel file system can be used and a file system adaptor provides a general POSIX-compliant interface. The Global Caching module maintains the connections between each cached data set and its parent copy. It coordinates with its peer on the remote site to move requested files according to user requests and to synchronize updates. The Global Caching module builds on top of the local native parallel file system by organizing the local storage space to maintain the duplicated copies of remote files. It intercepts local file requests and moves remote data transparently in case the requested file is not available locally. Therefore, it exposes the same POSIX-compliant file interface to applications. Accordingly, the global namespace is provided using the tree-based directory structure and seamlessly integrates into the namespace of local file system. The Consistency module coordinates the data synchronization according to user specified configurations.

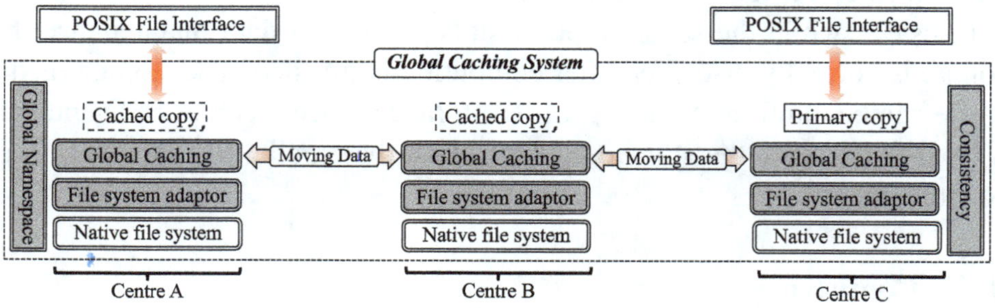

Fig. 3. Major components in the global caching architecture.

4 System Demonstrations

We are currently building a prototype of the global caching architecture for testing and evaluation purpose. We reuse existing file system components as much as possible to minimize the implementation effort. The caching system builds on GPFS [13], Active File Management (AFM) [17], and the NFS protocol [36]. We realized a platform-independent method to allocate, instantiate and release the caching instance with the target compute cluster across different IaaS clouds in an on-demand manner.

4.1 Existing Components

GPFS is a parallel file system designed for clusters, but behaves likes a general-purpose POSIX file system running on a single machine. GPFS uses the shared-disk architecture to achieve extreme scalability, and supports fully parallel access both to file data and metadata. Files are striped across all disks, while distributed locking synchronizes accesses to shared disks. Our caching system uses the GPFS product, (also known as IBM Spectrum Scale [16]), to hold both local and remote data sets.

As a component of IBM Spectrum Scale, AFM is a scalable, high-performance, clustered file system cache across a WAN. It provides a POSIX-compliant interface with disconnected operations, persistence across failures, and consistency management. AFM transfers data from remote file systems and tolerates latency across long haul networks using the NFS protocol. Parallel data transfer is supported with concurrent NFS connections.

Figure 4 illustrates an instance of the global caching site. The GPFS cluster provides data service to the compute cluster. Each GPFS cluster is equipped with an AFM component. Each server is attached multiple network shared disks. A configuration of mirror redundancy is shown in Fig. 4. The number of servers and associated disks depends on the total storage capacity needed. The number of gateway nodes determines the aggregated bandwidth that can be achieved to transfer data in and out from the cluster. Quorum managers maintain data consistency in the failure cases. The compute cluster consists of multiple workers and a job scheduler with a login node.

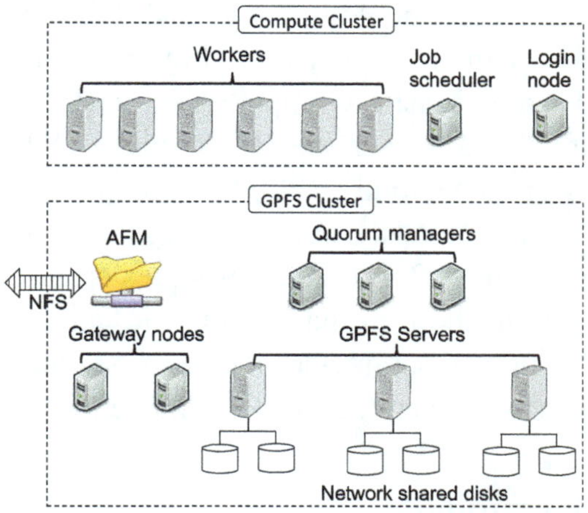

Fig. 4. An instance of the global caching site.

4.2 Platform-Independent System Resource Management

The global caching system aims to support different IaaS cloud systems and provides a platform-independent way of managing resource usage, including compute and storage resource allocation, instantiation and release. Our primitive implementation handles Amazon EC2, HUAWEI Public Cloud and OpenStack-based clouds. We realized a tool that supports different cloud orchestration methods, such as CloudFormation in EC2 and Heat in OpenStack and HUAWEI Cloud, to automate the allocation, release, and deployment of both compute and storage resources for building the caching site. To configure each virtual node and storage resources in an automated manner, we use Ansible [2] scripts. Both CloudFormation and Heat support Resource Tags to identify and categorize cloud resources. Our automation tool utilizes this feature to generate Ansible inventory and variables programmatically for system installation and configuration.

Table 1. Cloud resources in Amazon EC2, HUAWEI Cloud, and OpenStack.

Resources	Amazon EC2	HUAWEI Cloud	OpenStack
Virtual machine	Instance	Elastic Compute Server	Nova instance
OS images	AMI	Glance	Glance
Block storage	EBS	Elastic Volume Service	Cinder
Private network	VPC	VPC	Neutron network
Public IP	Public IP	Elastic IP	Floating IP
AAA	SSH key pairs	SSH key pairs	SSH key pairs

In order to accommodate a consistent caching system deployment over different clouds, according network resources, Authentication, access and authorization (AAA), virtual machines, and storage instances must be supported. Table 1 lists supported resources in Amazon EC2, HUAWEI Cloud, and OpenStack.

Figure 5 illustrates the typical deployment in both HUAWEI and Amazon clouds. In HUAWEI Cloud, shown in the left half of Fig. 5, both the compute and GPFS clusters are instantiated using Elastic Compute Server (ECS). Each GPFS server is attached with two Elastic Volume Service (EVS) disks. All of the ECS servers are connected with a Virtual Private Cloud (VPC) that communicates with the Internet via a NAT gateway. Each GPFS gateway node is equipped with an Elastic IP (EIP) to access the Internet directly. In EC2, different resources are used to provide the similar configuration, as illustrated in the right half of Fig. 5. Our automation tool allows for and accommodates configurable parameters for the type and number of instances as well as block devices attached, operating system image and other tunable parameters.

4.3 Data Transfer Optimization

Achieving high performance data transfer in a WAN requires tuning the components associated with the distant path, including storage devices and hosts in both source and destination sites and network connections [4, 8, 43]. Critical system parameters such as the TCP buffer size and the number of parallel data transfers in AFM must be optimized. In most cases, it is necessary to transfer the data with multiple Socket connections in order to utilize the bandwidth of the physical link efficiently. Besides moving multiple files concurrently, parallel data transfer must support file split to transfer a single large file. With AFM, parallel data transfer can be achieved at different levels: (1) multiple threads on a single gateway node; (2) multiple gateway nodes. Each option suits for different scenario. For example, in case the Network Interface Card (NIC) on a single gateway node provides enough bandwidth, the first option is enough. In case there is restriction on the NIC bandwidth, multiple gateway nodes can be used. AFM supports parallel data transfer with configurable parameters to adjust the number of concurrent read/write threads, and the size of chunk to split a huge file.

With Amazon EC2, we use a single gateway node with multiple threads to parallelize data transfer. However, with HUAWEI Cloud, each EIP has a bandwidth limitation. To maximize the performance of copying remote files, multiple gateway nodes are used in the cache site. Accordingly, in the home site the same number of NFS servers are deployed. The mapping between them is configured explicitly with AFM.

4.4 Data Consistency

The following data consistency modes are provided to coordinate concurrent data access across distant centers with the assistance of AFM:

- Read Only: each caching site can only read the cached copies, but cannot update them.
- Single Writer: only a single data site updates the cached file set, and the updates are synchronized to other caching sites automatically.

- Concurrent Writer: multiple writers update the same file with application layer coordination. The updates are synchronized without users interference.

AFM allows data to be cached at the block level, while data consistency is maintained per file. When reading or writing a file, only the accessed blocks are fetched into a local cache. When the file is closed, the dirty blocks are written to the local file system and synchronized remotely to ensure a consistent state of the file.

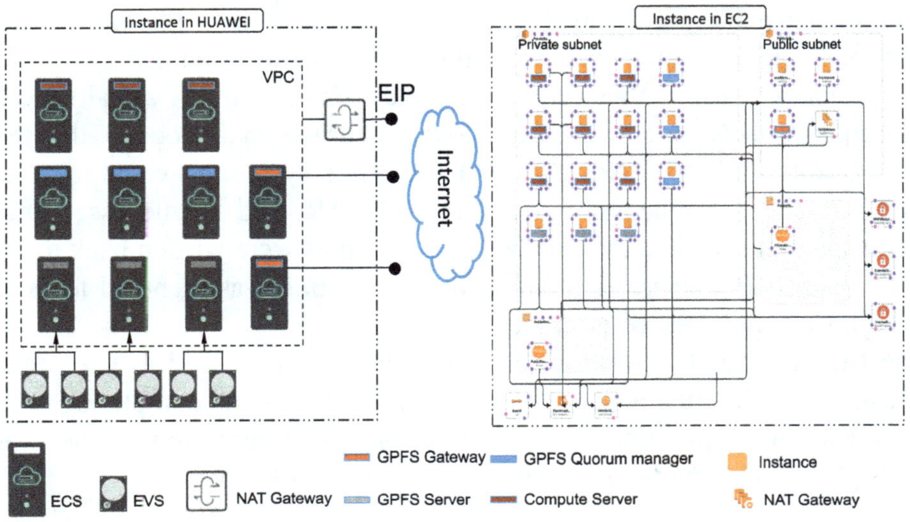

Fig. 5. The deployment of a caching instance in HUAWEI Cloud and Amazon EC2.

5 Case Study and Performance Evaluation

We use a Genome Wide Association Study (GWAS) as an application driver to show how to use our global caching architecture to assist on-demand scientific computing across different clouds. GWAS are hypothesis-free methods to identify associations between regions of the genome and complex traits and disease. This analysis was performed on data from the Systems Genomics of Parkinson's Disease consortium, which has collected DNA methylation data on about 2,000 individuals. This study aimed to test how genetic variation alters DNA methylation, an epigenetic modification that controls how genes are expressed, while the results are being used to understand the biological pathways through which genetic variation affects disease risk.

The work totally conducts 3.3×10^{12} statistical tests using the PLINK software [35]. The workload is essentially embarrassingly parallel and does not require high performance communication across virtual machines within the cloud. The data to be analyzed, around 40 GB in total, is stored in NeCTAR's data collection storage site located in the campus of the University of Queensland (UQ) at Brisbane. The input data is moved to the virtualized clusters, acquired in Amazon EC2 and HUAWEI Cloud, as requested. In addition, we can control the size of the cloud resource, for both the compute and GPFS clusters, according to our testing requirements.

5.1 System Deployment

As shown in Fig. 6, virtualized compute clusters acquired from EC2 and HUAWEI clouds respectively process input data stored in Brisbane. Each instance, including both compute and GPFS clusters, is created using the automation tool described previously. The size of each instance was selected to make the best usage of our available credit. The EC2 instance is created with a single VPC located in Sydney availability zone. The HUAWEI instance consists of two layers. The first layer is a caching only site located in Beijing and the second layer consists of both caching and compute clusters located in Shanghai. The EC2 and HUAWEI resources connected to the central storage site in Brisbane via the global caching architecture. The data transferred between these data sites is achieved using NFS connections and AFM caching. Typically, AFM NSD protocol outperforms NFS. However, due to the security concern occurred in the public network, we could only use NFS. The global caching system provided local access to data even though it was actually stored in NeCTAR, and the necessary files were fetched transparently on demand. Likewise, output files were written back to NeCTAR without the user being aware. Therefore, the application was identical to as if it was executed on a local cluster without any modification.

In the EC2 cluster, the Nimrod [11] job scheduler was used to execute 500,000 PLINK tasks, spreading the load across the compute nodes and completing the work in three days. Overall, approximately 60 TBs of data were generated by the experiment and sent back to Brisbane for long-term storage and post-processing.

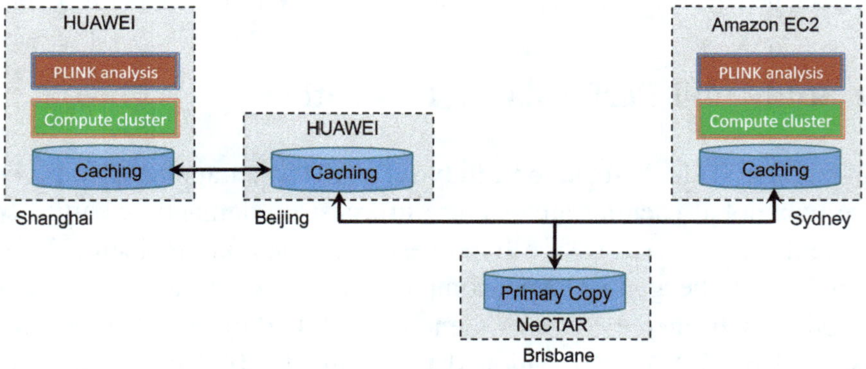

Fig. 6. The deployment of the global caching architecture for GWAS case study.

With the hierarchical caching structure in HUAWEI cloud, the input data was moved from Australia to Beijing first and then copied to Shanghai center. Due to credit limitation, no significant compute jobs were executed in HUAWEI Cloud.

5.2 AWS EC2 Instance Selection

We investigated the appropriate AWS instance for our EC2 experiment. Due to the constraints of time and cost, we could not exhaustively explore all the available instances. We used a holistic approach to identify which instance types provide optimal performance for different roles. Briefly, with the option of network-attached storage, instance types, such as *m4*, could not provide sufficient EBS bandwidth for GPFS Servers. Therefore, we examined the instances associated with the ephemeral storage of local block devices. However, the *d2* series, namely the *d2.8xlarge* type, experienced hardware and underlying infrastructure reliability issues. Finally, we used the *i3* instance types, *i3.16xlarge*, for the GPFS cluster that provided 25 Gbit/sec network with the ephemeral NVMe class storage, and had no reliability issues. For the compute cluster, we selected the compute-optimized flavours, *c5.9xlarge*. It had a dedicated 10 Gbit/sec bandwidth with Intel Xeon Skylake CPUs.

Table 2. Configurations of Amazon EC2 testing.

Type of nodes	Instances	Count	Details
Nimrod worker	c5.9xlarge	25	750 Xeon Skylake cores in total
AFM gateway	i3.16xlarge	2	Each instance is equipped with
GPFS quorum	i3.16xlarge	3	25 Gbit/sec network bandwidth
GPFS server	i3.16xlarge	10	and 8 $\times$ 1.9 TB NVME

To determine instance counts, we matched aggregated worker bandwidth to GPFS Server bandwidth to satisfy a fully balanced IO path. Further, we tested a small scale of the PLINK workload to estimate run time per job and then sized our virtual cluster to execute the full workload within $\sim$3 days. The final configuration is listed in Table 2. Totally, 750 Nimrod worker threads were launched on the compute cluster.

5.3 Network Transfer Optimization

The network between AWS Sydney and UQ is 10 Gbps with around 18.5 ms latency. The connection is under a peering arrangement between the national research network provider, AARNET, and Amazon. The network is shared with other academic and research sector AARNET partners. Therefore, our configuration aims to maximize the effective bandwidth. For this case, a single active gateway node was used with 32 AFM read/write threads at the cache site. In comparison, the default option is just one read/write thread. TCP buffers were tuned to improve performance at both source and destination sites. The home NFS server currently serves production workloads and requires 4,096 NFS daemons to service this workload. With these optimizations in place, we achieved about 2 Gbps, which is 20% of the peak bandwidth on the shared public link. The total amount of data moved from UQ to Amazon Sydney was 40 GB, but the amount of data moved back to our datacenter (home) was 60 TB in total.

5.4 Performance Evaluation

During the 3 days of experiment, system utilization was on average about 85–92% on each node, with the I/O peaking at about 420,000 output and 25,000 input operations per second (IOPS). The total 500,000 tasks were launched in 5 batches sequentially. This allowed us to optimize the system configuration while monitoring the progress of computing and expense used. Actually, the system was tuned in the first batch. Therefore, we only present the performance statistics for the last 4 batches. We used the EC2 CloudWatch tools to monitor the performance. In particular, we captured CPU utilization, network traffic and IOPS for each instance.

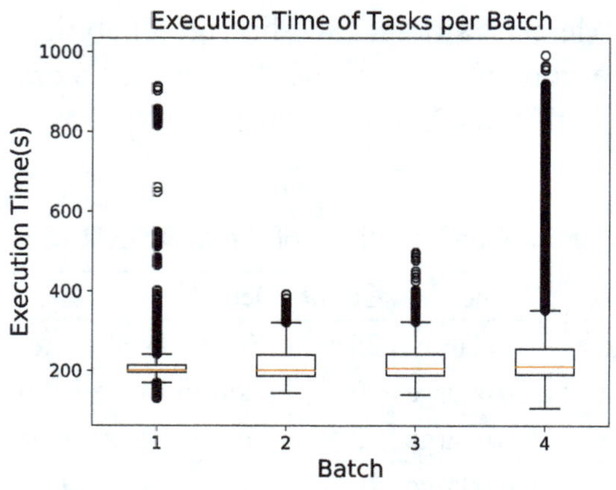

Fig. 7. Performance variation of PLINK tasks.

Although each PLINK task consists of similar computational complexity with almost same size of input data, we observed significant performance variation, as illustrated in Fig. 7. The averaged execution time is 200 s with a long tail of outliers, and some special cases could take up to 1,000 s. Commonly, performance variability exists in a large scale of distributed system. Shared resources and system and network instability can lead to huge performance variation [3]. For our case, we observed significant variations of IO access for PLINK tasks.

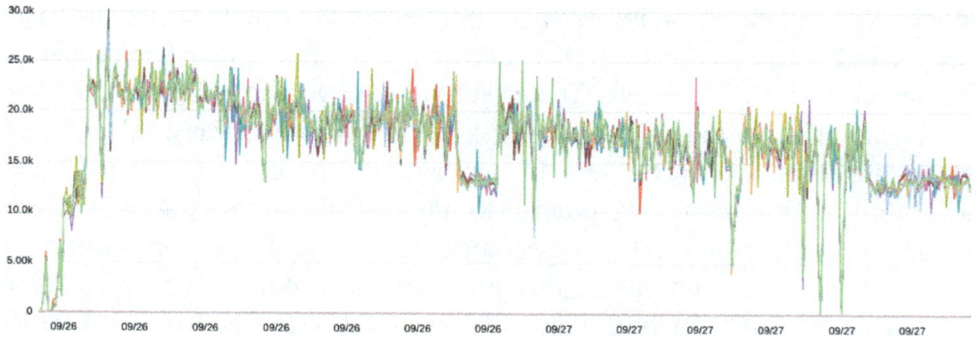

Fig. 8. Disk read operations per second. (Color figure online)

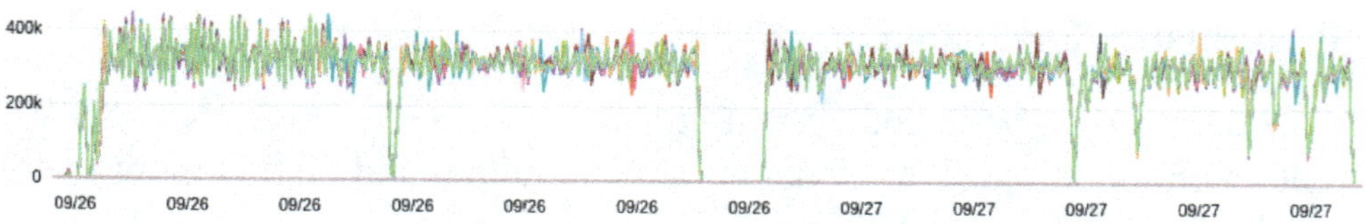

Fig. 9. Disk write operations per second. (Color figure online)

Fig. 10. Outbound network traffic of AFM gateway nodes. (Color figure online)

Figures 8 and 9 show the disk read and write statistics for compute servers, in which each line with different color represents metrics for a single instance. Because of the PLINK workload, write IO is an order of magnitude higher than read performance. The metrics of different instances are correlated very well and it means the workload on each instance is pretty similar. In particular, the write performance was comparatively stable within the range of 200K and 400K. We believe this is because the updates were first committed to local NVMe devices before being transferred to the home site through AFM gateway. In comparison, averaged read operations changes from around 22K to less 15K. This may be caused by unreliable long-haul network.

Figure 10 presents the network traffic from Amazon to UQ through GPFS gateway at the caching site, in which the orange line represents the operative gateway node and the blue one is for the fail-over backup node. We can see that most remote data traffics were managed by the operative gateway node. There are significant drops in the last day of experiment. We assume they were caused by shared bandwidth competition from other public users. This resource contention also impacts the PLINK execution time at the last day, especially the performance of read IO.

6 Conclusions

Geographically distributed data processing pipelines are becoming common. The stages of data intensive analysis can be accelerated using cloud computing with the high throughput model and on-demand resource allocation. It is desired that existing parallel applications can be offloaded into a multi-cloud environment without significant modifications. To achieve this goal, this paper presents a global caching architecture that provides a uniform storage solution to migrate data sets across different clouds transparently. In particular, on-demand data movement is provided by taking advantage of both temporal and spatial locality in geographical data pipelines. Cooperating with the dynamic resource allocation, our system can improve the efficiency of large-scale data pipelines in multi-clouds. Our architecture provides a hierarchical caching framework with a tree structure and the global namespace using the POSIX file interface. The system is demonstrated by combining existing storage software, including GPFS, AFM, and NFS. Parallel IO is supported directly to improve the performance of scalable data analysis applications. Both block-based caching and file-based data consistency are supported in the global domain. A platform independent method is realized to allocate, instantiate and release the caching site with both compute and storage clusters across different clouds. The case study of GWAS demonstrates that our system can organize public resources from IaaS clouds, such as both Amazon EC2 and HUAWEI Cloud, in a uniform way to accelerate massive bioinformatics data analysis. In particular, the PLINK analysis was offloaded into the multi-cloud environment without any modification and worked as if it was executed on a local cluster. The performance evaluation demonstrates that our global caching architecture has successfully addressed its design goals.

Acknowledgments. We thank Amazon and HUAWEI for contributing cloud resources to this research project.

References

1. Amazon S3 Homepage. https://aws.amazon.com/s3/. Accessed 30 Nov 2018
2. Ansible Homepage. https://www.ansible.com/. Accessed 30 Nov 2018
3. Dean, J., Barroso, L.: The tail at scale. Commun. ACM **56**, 74–80 (2013)
4. Kumar, A., et al.: BwE: flexible, hierarchical bandwidth allocation for WAN distributed computing. In: Proceedings of the 2015 ACM Conference on Special Interest Group on Data Communication (SIGCOMM 2015), London (2015)
5. Rajendran, A., et al.: Optimizing large data transfers over 100Gbps wide area network. In: Proceedings of 13th IEEE/ACM International Symposium on Cluster, Cloud, and Grid Computing (CCGrid 2013), Delft (2013)
6. Thomson, A., Abadi, D.J.: CalvinFS: consistent WAN replication and scalable metadata management for distributed file systems. In: Proceeding of the 13th USENIX Conference on File and Storage Techniques (FAST 2015), CA (2015)
7. Allen, B., et al.: Globus online: radical simplification of data movement via SaaS. Technical report, The University of Chicago (2011)
8. Settlemyer, B., et al.: A technique for moving large data sets over high-performance long distance networks. In: Proceedings of IEEE 27th Symposium on Mass Storage Systems and Technologies (MSST 2011), Denver (2011)
9. Dropbox Homepage. https://www.dropbox.com. Accessed 30 Nov 2018
10. Abramson, D., Carroll, J., Jin, C., Mallon, M.: A metropolitan area infrastructure for data intensive science. In: Proceedings of IEEE 13th International Conference on e-Science (e-Science), Auckland (2017)
11. Abramson, D., Sosic, R., Giddy, J., Hall, B.: Nimrod: a tool for performing parametrised simulations using distributed workstations. In: Proceedings of the 4th IEEE International Symposium on High Performance Distributed Computing (1995)
12. Nygren, E., Sitaraman, R., Sun, J.: The Akamai network: a platform for high-performance internet applications. ACM SIGOPS Oper. Syst. Rev. Arch. **44**(3), 2–19 (2010)
13. Schmuck, F., Haskin, R.: GPFS: a shared-disk file system for large computing clusters. In: Proceedings of the 1st USENIX Conference on File and Storage Techniques (FAST) (2002)
14. Hupfeld, F., et al.: The XtreemFS architecture: a case for object-based file systems in grids. J. Concurr. Comput. **20**(17), 2049–2060 (2008)

15. Khanna, G., et al.: Using overlays for efficient data transfer over shared wide-area networks. In: Proceedings of the 2008 ACM/IEEE Conference on Supercomputing (SC 2008), Austin (2008)
16. IBM Spectrum Scale Homepage. https://www.ibm.com/support/knowledgecenter/en/STXKQY_4.2.0. Accessed 30 Nov 2018
17. IBM, Active File Management (AFM) Homepage. https://www.ibm.com/support/knowledgecenter/en/STXKQY_4.2.0/com.ibm.spectrum.scale.v4r2.adv.doc/bl1adv_afm.htm. Accessed 30 Nov 2018
18. Reuter, H.: Direct client access to vice partitions. In: AFS & Kerberos Best Practice Workshop 2009, CA (2009)
19. Raicu, I., et al.: The quest for scalable support of data-intensive workloads in distributed systems. In: Proceedings of the 18th ACM International Symposium on High performance Distributed Computing (HPDC 2009), Munich (2009)
20. Raicu, I., Zhao, Y., Foster, I., Szalay, A.: Accelerating large-scale data exploration through data diffusion. In: IEEE International Workshop on Data-Aware Distributed Computing (DADC 2008) (2008)
21. Bent, J., et al.: Explicit control in a batch-aware distributed file system. In: Proceedings of the 1st Conference on Symposium on Networked Systems Design and Implementation (NSDI 2004), CA (2004)
22. Corbett, J., et al.: Spanner: Google's globally distributed database. ACM Trans. Comput. Syst. (TOCS) **31**(3–8), 1–22 (2013)
23. Kubiatowicz, J., et al.: OceanStore: an architecture for global-scale persistent storage. In: Proceedings of the 9th International Conference on Architectural Support for Programming Languages and Operating Systems (ASPLOS) (2000)
24. Morris, J., et al.: Andrew: a distributed personal computing environment. Commun. ACM-MIT Press Sci. Comput. Ser. **29**(3), 184–201 (1986)
25. Vahi, K., et al.: Rethinking data management for big data scientific workflows. In: Proceedings of 2013 IEEE International Conference on Big Data, Silicon Valley (2013)
26. Biven, L.: Big data at the department of energy's office of science. In: 2nd NIST Big Data Public Working Group Workshop (2017)
27. Pacheco, L., et al.: GlobalFS: a strongly consistent multi-site file system. In: Proceedings of IEEE 35th Symposium on Reliable Distributed Systems (SRDS), Budapest (2016)
28. Vitale, M.: OpenAFS cache manager performance. In: AFS & Kerberos Best Practice Workshop 2015, PA (2015)
29. Microsoft Azure Homepage. https://azure.microsoft.com/en-us/. Accessed 30 Nov 2018
30. Hey, T., Tansley, S., Tolle, K.: The Fourth Paradigm: Data-Intensive Scientific Discovery. Microsoft Corporation, Redmond (2012)
31. Eshel, M., Haskin, R., Hildebrand, D., Naik, M., Schmuck, F., Tewari, R.: Panache: a parallel file system cache for global file access. In: Proceedings of the 8th USENIX Conference on File and Storage Technologies (FAST 2010), California (2010)
32. Ardekani, M., Terry, D.: A self-configurable geo-replicated cloud storage system. In: Proceedings of the 11th USENIX Conference on Operating Systems Design and Implementation (OSDI 2014) (2014)
33. Nextcloud Homepage. https://nextcloud.com. Accessed 30 Nov 2018
34. OpenAFS Homepage. https://www.openafs.org/. Accessed 31 Jan 2019
35. PLINK Homepage. http://zzz.bwh.harvard.edu/plink/. Accessed 30 Nov 2018
36. Sandberg, R., Goldberg, D., Kleiman, S., Walsh, D., Lyon, B.: Design and implementation of the sun network file system. In: Proceedings of the Summer USENIX (1985)
37. Tudoran, R., Costan, A., Antoniu, G.: OverFlow: multi-site aware big data management for scientific workflows on clouds. IEEE Trans. Cloud Comput. **4**(1), 76–89 (2016)

38. Tudoran, R., Costan, A., Rad, R., Brasche, G., Antoniu, G.: Adaptive file management for scientific workflows on the Azure cloud. In: Proceedings of 2013 IEEE International Conference on Big Data, Silicon Valley (2013)
39. Tudoran, R., Costan, A., Wang, R., Bouge, L., Antoniu, G.: Bridging data in the clouds: an environment-aware system for geographically distributed data transfers. In: Proceedings of 14th IEEE/ACM International Symposium on Cluster, Cloud, and Grid Computing (CCGrid 2014), Delft (2013)
40. Dolev, S., Florissi, P., Gudes, E., Sharma, S., Singer, I.: A survey on geographically distributed big-data processing using MapReduce. IEEE Trans. Big Data **5**(1), 60–80 (2017)
41. Rhea, S., et al.: Pond: the OceanStore prototype. In: Proceedings of the 2nd USENIX Conference on File and Storage Technologies (FAST 2003) (2003)
42. Allcock, W.: GridFTP: protocol extensions to FTP for the grid. Global Grid ForumGFD-R-P.020 (2003)
43. Kim, Y., Atchley, S., Vallee, G., Shipman, G.: LADS: optimizing data transfers using layout-aware data scheduling. In: Proceedings of the 13th USENIX Conference on File and Storage Technologies (FAST 2015), Santa Clara (2015)
44. Wu, Z., et al.: SPANStore: cost-effective geo-replicated storage spanning multiple cloud services. In: Proceedings of the 24th ACM Symposium on Operating Systems Principles (SOSP 2013) (2013)

PHINEAS: An Embedded Heterogeneous Parallel Platform

Nikhil Khatri(✉), Nithin Bodanapu(✉), and T. S. B. Sudarshan(✉)

Department of Computer Science and Engineering,
PES University, Bangalore 560085, India
nikhilkhatri97@gmail.com, nithinbodanapu97@gmail.com,
sudarshan.tsb@gmail.com

Abstract. With machine learning being applied to increasingly varied domains, the computational needs of researchers have increased proportionately. Hobbyists, researchers and universities are turning to building their own cluster computers to meet their high performance compute needs. These clusters are typically highly efficient, low cost ARM based platforms consisting of between 4 and 8 nodes. In this paper, we present PHINEAS: Parallel Heterogeneous INdigenous Embedded ARM System, a parallel compute platform which allows for distributed computation using MPI and OpenMP and which further leverages the on-board GPU to perform general purpose compute tasks. We describe the hardware components of the cluster, the software stack installed on each node and a host of common benchmark algorithms and their results. The results show that the cluster meets the stringent latency requirements of embedded systems. We further describe how the on-board GPU's OpenGL ES 2.0 programming model can be used to implement tasks such as image convolution and neural network inference which are common in intelligent embedded systems. Parallelisation of compute tasks across multiple GPUs is discussed as a method to combine the advantages of distributed and heterogeneous computing.

Keywords: Cluster computer · Embedded system · Heterogenous computer

1 Introduction

The class of platform that PHINEAS belongs to is frequently referred to as a Beowulf cluster [16]. These are described as "scalable performance clusters based on commodity hardware, on a private system network, with open source software (Linux) infrastructure" [12]. Common configurations typically include multiple nodes with the same hardware. This may be either the same processor, or, as in our case, the identical computer. Modern Beowulf clusters frequently make use of a class of computers titled SBCs (Single Board Computers). These include a processor, GPU, RAM, storage and I/O such as USB, ethernet and wireless communication all on one board. Most common clusters consist of anywhere

D. Abramson and B. R. de Supinski (Eds.): SCFA 2019, LNCS 11416, pp. 57–70, 2019.
https://doi.org/10.1007/978-3-030-18645-6_4

between 2 and 16 boards [1,15]. Extreme examples which consist of hundreds of nodes also exist. The RaspberryPi has emerged as the most commonly used SBC for Beowulf clusters. Its low cost, easy availability, power efficiency and excellent support make it a popular choice. Most literature on existing embedded parallel platforms provide data about performance scaling across nodes for common compute tasks such as matrix multiplication, image convolution and algorithms such as mergesort. However, there seems to have been little work done towards utilizing the GPUs on such boards for general compute tasks. To this end, we built **PHINEAS: Parallel Heterogeneous INdigenous Embedded ARM System**. This was one of the primary goals of our research: to use the on-board GPU to perform compute tasks.

2 Hardware and Construction

Any cluster like PHINEAS consists of three main components. Namely, the compute board, the power supply and the networking hardware. The power supply is usually dictated by the power draw associated with each board and the total number of boards in the cluster. The network switch must match the bandwidth afforded by the SBC and must provide enough ports to accommodate all boards and extra lines for extra-net connections.

2.1 Single Board Computer

The SBC chosen for the cluster affects performance more than any other part. When considering boards we used the following factors to guide our choice:

CPU. The CPU plays a lead role in all the computation done on the cluster. When comparing board CPUs, clock speed and number of cores play a critical role. Most of the boards considered had a clock speed greater than or equal to 1 GHz. Boards in this class typically have between 2 and 4 cores, with the rare exception having 8 cores. The number of cores defines the amount of parallelism we would be able to extract on each board using OpenMP.

GPU. The GPU is more important for our cluster than most other clusters since GPGPU compute is an important goal for us. However, this was not a critical point when making a choice since most boards have the same MALI 400 MP2 GPU clocked at around 500 MHz. A notable exception is the Raspberry Pi 3B+ which has a Broadcom GPU.

RAM. All boards we considered had 1 GB of RAM. This is critical for most applications which rely on data level parallelism since large data sets must be kept in memory and accessed frequently. Other than the Raspberry Pi, all boards have DDR3 RAM. The Raspberry Pi has the slower LPDDR2 generation of RAM.

Networking. Networking is typically a significant overhead in distributed computing. To minimize this overhead it is essential that a high bandwidth ethernet port is offered by the board. Most boards offer ethernet ports with gigabit speeds. A notable exception was the Raspberry Pi which has a maximum speed of about 300 Mbps [10].

Power. Since one of the key features of a embedded parallel platform is efficiency, low power draw for each component is a must. Most boards that we considered did not deviate significantly from the 5 Volt/2 Ampere mark.

Storage. An often neglected feature of these SBCs is the storage options offered by them. This is because seldom do these boards offer more than a single SDcard slot. An alternate option is eMMC memory. This may either be soldered onboard, or be connected as an external module. eMMC memory has much higher read throughput than an SD card and also has better write resiliency [11]. Storage sizes typically range between 8 GB and 32 GB, with 8 being the minimum required for most operating systems.

Chosen Board. Keeping these factors in mind, we selected the NanoPi M1 Plus for our cluster [7]. This was chosen for its gigabit networking, 1 GB of DDR3 RAM and most importantly, 8 GB of eMMC storage. The board has a Allwinner H3 SOC, which has a quad-core Cortex-A7 CPU and a Mali-400 MP2 GPU. The availability of the board in India contributed strongly to our choice. Other boards we considered were the Raspberry Pi 3B+ [10], the Pine A64+[9] and the NanoPi Fire 3 [6]. It is important to note that our decision was based on the specifications of the various boards and the data provided by others. We did not benchmark these boards ourselves (Table 1).

2.2 Power Supply

For powering the entire cluster it is necessary that the chosen power supply is able to provide sufficient voltage to each node while also being able to provide the necessary total wattage of the cluster. A stable power source is hence necessary for consistent operation. We chose to use two 5-port USB hubs, each of which provides up to 40 W of power which is sufficient for 4 boards.

2.3 Network Switch

For communication among the nodes of the cluster it is essential to have a switch that can make use of the gigabit ethernet ports on the compute boards so as to avoid any network latency during computation. This trend is common in clusters where the boards support full gigabit networking [1]. Another technology available for ethernet is PoE - Power over Ethernet. This allows us to fuse the power delivery and networking into a single connection backbone. The drawback of this is, that it limits gigabit connection to 100 Mbps, since the remaining lines are used for power delivery. Further, of the boards we considered, only the raspberry pi 3b+ supports PoE. Even this requires a special PoE HAT (Hardware Attached on Top) and a PoE capable switch which are typically more expensive.

2.4 PHINEAS Specification

The PHINEAS cluster consists of two stacks, each consisting of 4 NanoPi M1 Plus boards, with a 8-port gigabit switch and a USB power supply rated at 40W. Each stack has approximate dimensions 35 cm × 25 cm × 25 cm, making it suitable for embedded systems. The cluster has no moving parts and is thus structurally stable. If the eMMC storage is used as the boot partition, the microSD card can also be removed, resulting in a system without any loose components.

Table 1. Board specification comparison

Feature	Raspberry Pi 3 B+	Pine A64+	NanoPi Fire3	NanoPi M1 Plus
Processor	Broadcom CortexA53 (1.4 GHz) x 4	Cortex A53 (1.2 GHz) x 4	S5P6818 (1.4 GHz) x 8	Cortex A7 (1.2 GHz) x 4
GPU	Broadcom Videocore 4	Mali 400 MP2	Mali 400 MP4	Mali 400 MP2
RAM	1 GB LPDDR2	1 GB DDR3	1 GB DDR3	1 GB DDR3
Ethernet	Gigabit (300 Mbps)	Gigabit	Gigabit	Gigabit
Power draw	5 V/2.5 A	5 V/2 A	5 V/2 A	5 V/2 A
Storage	microSD	microSD	microSD	eMMC + microSD

3 Software Stack

In our cluster, we reserved one board for research involving the GPU and the remaining were used for the tests described in the next section. This is because the manufacturer recommends a different OS distribution when writing code for the GPU. Note: There are no hardware differences between the boards. For the 7 benchmark boards, we installed Linux 4.14 based on the mainline kernel. This was provided by FriendlyARM, the board manufacturer. For parallel programming within the board, we installed OpenMP. For distributing work across boards, we installed MPICH3 which is an implementation of the Message Passing Interface. This provides an easy to use API when distributing workloads across multiple machines connected over a network.

To use the GPU, we installed the Linux-3.4 OS image which was provided by Allwinner, the manufacturer of the SOC.

4 Performance Benchmarks

As described in the previous section OpenMP and MPI were used to distribute the workload across the cluster. Various common algorithms were run on the PHINEAS cluster using 1, 2 .. 7 nodes incrementally. The time taken for each execution was recorded and plotted against number of nodes used. This provides us with an understanding of the speedup achieved for various workloads. The programs suitably exert the CPU, memory and networking of the cluster and its computers.

4.1 Monte Carlo Pi Estimation

Monte Carlo Pi estimation is a method to estimate the value of pi based on randomly generated values [5]. It calculates the ratio of number of points lying inside a circle against the number of points lying inside a square. We run multiple iterations to randomly generate points in two dimensional space and to parallelize it we distribute a chunk of iterations to each node. This test was done solely to show that for a large enough problem size we can achieve close to ideal speed up. In our case it was 6.89 for a 7 node cluster. The speedup graph obtained on PHINEAS is provided in Fig. 1. The X-axes shows the number of nodes used to distribute the workload of 1000000, 10000000 and 100000000 iterations to estimate Pi.

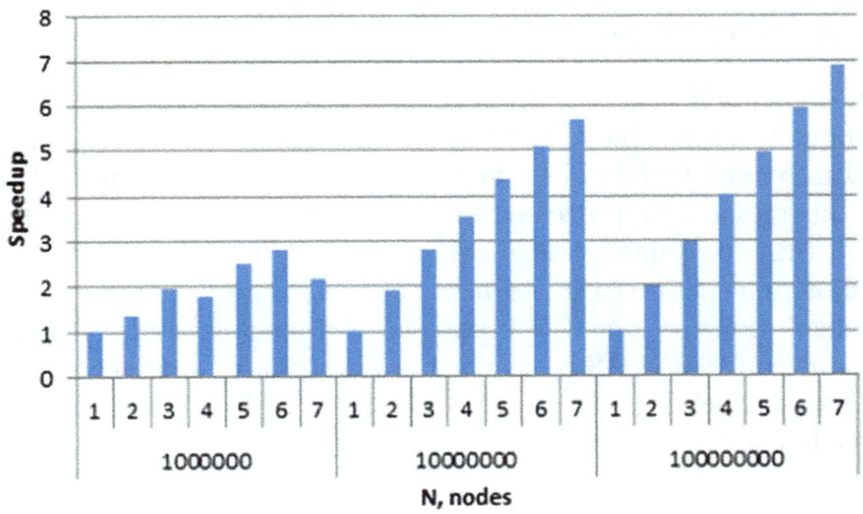

Fig. 1. Speedup observed for distributed Monte Carlo Pi estimation

4.2 Distributed Merge Sort

Merge sort is a simple sorting algorithm that has the added advantage of easily being parallelisable. The reason for using this as a benchmark is that it is a common algorithm that places a heavy load on the network as it requires the scatter and gather of large array chunks across all the nodes of a cluster. The speedup graph obtained on PHINEAS is provided in Fig. 2. The x-axis shows the number of nodes used to distribute the workload of N (10000, 100000 and 1000000) elements in the array which is to be sorted. An existing C implementation using MPI was used [3].

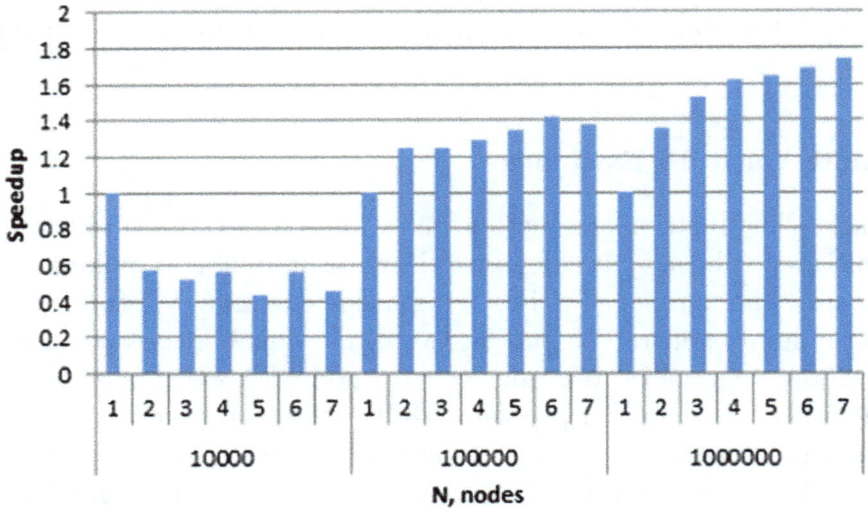

Fig. 2. Speedup observed for distributed Merge Sort

4.3 Image Convolution

One of the main applications for this cluster was robotics which involves frequent use of computer vision. One of the main tasks in computer vision is image convolution. Images can be convolved in an immensely parallel manner, where each pixel can theoretically be processed in parallel. The benchmark program works by dividing the image into vertical columns, applying the convolution filter on each of these and merging the segments of the image to get the final output. For the convolution the OpenCV library for Python was used [2]. The speedup graph obtained on PHINEAS is provided in Fig. 3. The X-axis shows the number of nodes across which the image to be convolved is distributed in a column by column fashion.

4.4 Hybrid Matrix Multiplication

We explored a hybrid approach of using OpenMP and MPI. This allowed us to parallelize workload across a cluster and also across all the cores of a processor, making full use of our Quad-Core CPUs. This is known to be an ideal method to distribute workload and optimize resources utilization. For a problem of $A \times B$ we send the matrix B to all the nodes and send a subset of rows of A to each node of the cluster. Within each node we compute the multiplication of rows to each column of B. Here there is scope for parallelization so that a row in A can

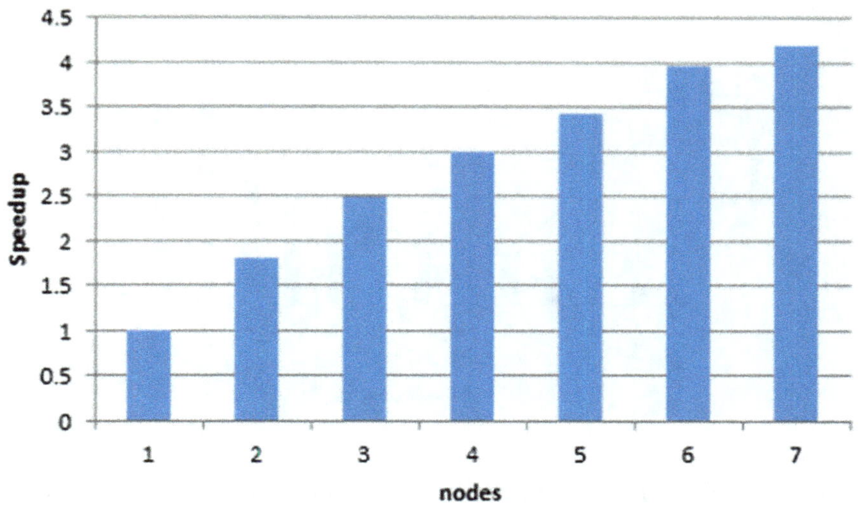

Fig. 3. Speedup observed for distributed image convolution

be multiplied by different columns of B simultaneously using multiple threads. This allows us to efficiently utilize all the resources available to us. In Figs. 4 and 5 we show the speedup obtained when using a single thread and multiple threads [4]. The X-axis shows the distribution of workload across the 7 nodes of PHINEAS with 1 and 4 threads used per node. The tabular form of the same data is given in Table 2.

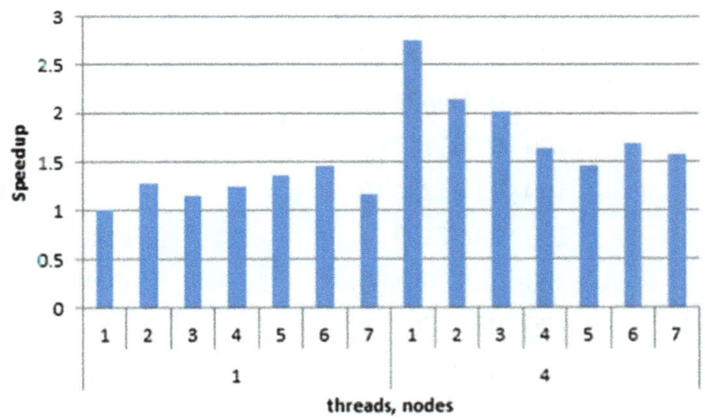

Fig. 4. Speedup observed for hybrid matrix multiplication with size of the matrices as 100×100

4.5 Neural Network Training

Deep Learning is one of the most researched areas in current times and is highly compute intensive and parallelisable. Taking this into consideration we parallelized an existing dense neural network built on python using the numpy library to train on the MNIST dataset. This network was parallelized using pyMPIch,

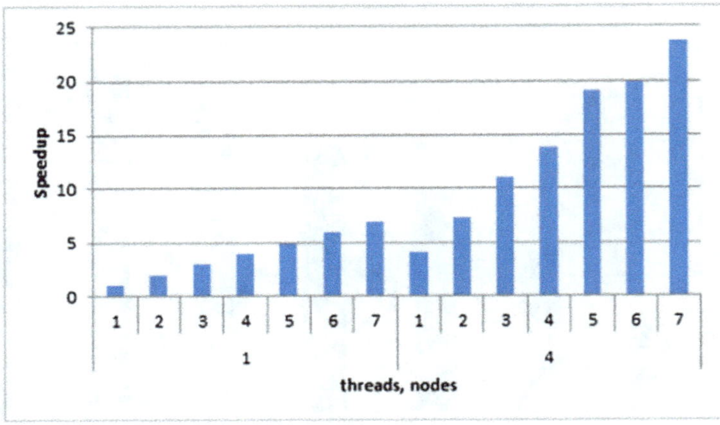

Fig. 5. Speedup observed for hybrid matrix multiplication with size of the matrices as 1000×1000

Table 2. Time for matrix multiplication under varying sizes and constraints like Matrix size, number of threads and number of nodes

Nodes	Threads	N	Time	Nodes	Threads	N	Time
1	1	100	0.109478	1	1	1000	159.870361
2	1	100	0.085684	2	1	1000	79.573329
3	1	100	0.095737	3	1	1000	53.578156
4	1	100	0.087392	4	1	1000	40.160633
5	1	100	0.080584	5	1	1000	32.261839
6	1	100	0.075198	6	1	1000	26.876678
7	1	100	0.094543	7	1	1000	23.273858
1	4	100	0.039621	1	4	1000	39.305208
2	4	100	0.051147	2	4	1000	21.83931
3	4	100	0.054234	3	4	1000	14.459377
4	4	100	0.067129	4	4	1000	11.512601
5	4	100	0.07509	5	4	1000	8.369552
6	4	100	0.064968	6	4	1000	8.057398
7	4	100	0.069967	7	4	1000	6.747061

a wrapper for the MPI library implemented in C. Hardware used for efficient training of neural networks involves the use of expensive GPUs especially for large complex networks. Such hardware is typically expensive and not easily available. Our aim is to provide a cost effective solution to this problem. The benchmark that we ran was of a dense neural network tested with 25, 50, 75 and 100 hidden units and we have seen that the speedup increases as the number of hidden units increases [8]. The idea behind showcasing this as a benchmark is to show how we can make use of a simple embedded system to reduce training time in a neural network. The speedup graph is given in Fig. 6. The X-axis consists of number of nodes the workload is distributed across different number of hidden units in the neural network.

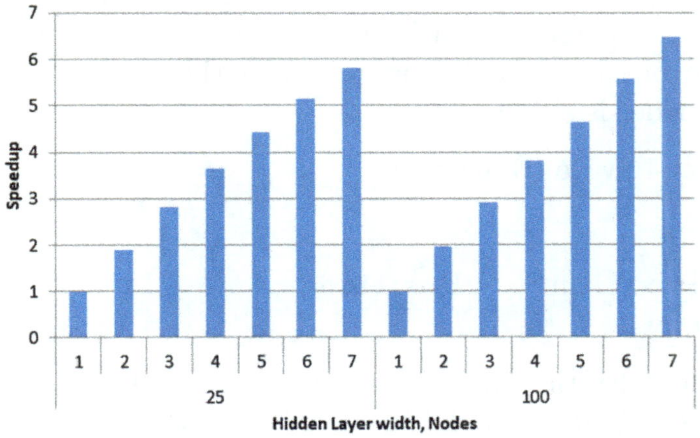

Fig. 6. Speedup observed for distributed dense neural network training with 25 hidden units

5 Graphics Processing Unit

A key goal of our project was to use the on-board GPU to perform general purpose computation, since this has not been achieved by any cluster of this class previously. The GPU on the NanoPi M1 Plus is the Mali-400 MP2. This, being a slightly older and lower performance GPU does not support modern programming environments such as OpenCL. This greatly hampers the ability to carry out non-graphical computation on the board. The API supported by the GPU is OpenGL ES 2.0 which is described in greater detail in the following subsection.

5.1 OpenGL ES 2.0

OpenGL ES is a cross-platform API for rendering 2D and 3D graphics on embedded and mobile systems. The 2.0 variant was the first API to support programmable shaders for a mobile or embedded environment [13]. When writing a program using OpenGL ES 2.0, output is controlled primarily through the two shaders: the vertex shader and the fragment shader.

Vertex Shader. The input to the vertex shader is a set of vertex attribute objects. One vertex is provided as input to each instance of the vertex shader. Each vertex consists of 4 attributes, representing location in x, y and z coordinates, and a fourth coordinate used for projection and transformations. The vertex shader is responsible for transforming or re-positioning the input vertex and providing a single transformed output vertex. On the Mali-400 MP2 there is one physical vertex shader. For our purposes, we do not perform any computation in the vertex shader. We simply provide the vertices of two triangles, which between them cover the entire screen.

Programming for both shaders is done using GLSL ES (OpenGL Shading Language), a C-like language which provides data types, mathematical operations and inbuilt variables to aid in programming the shaders [13]. Example code for the vertex shader is shown.

```
attribute vec4 vPosition;

void main() {
        gl_Position = vPosition;
}
```

vPosition provides the input vertex coordinates. These are simply copied over to *gl_Position*, which is the variable where the output vertex must be placed for each vertex shader instance.

Fragment Shader. After the vertex shader, the primitive shapes undergo rasterization to generate fragments, each of which has a specific depth and color value. It is the fragment shader's responsibility to color each fragment using its coordinates in the window and other optional variables such as textures and samplers.

On the Mali-400 MP2 there are 2 physical fragment shaders. This is where we perform the majority of our computation. A simple example of a fragment shader is shown.

```
void main(){
        gl_FragColor = vec4(1.0, 0, 0, 1.0);
}
```

This shader simply colors all fragments red. The *gl_FragColor* variable expects an output in RGBA form (Red, Green, Blue and Alpha) [13].

5.2 Image Convolution

One task which easily lends itself to GPU computation is image convolution. Convolution involves performing a matrix product of a given kernel (or convolution matrix) with each mxm submatrix of the image. Kernels may be 1D, 2D or 3D in cases where color is also used. This task is inherently parallel since the kernel can be applied to each submatrix of the image independently. To perform this task, the first challenge is how to provide an image to the fragment shader, where we intend to perform our computation. To do this, we make use of a feature of OpenGL called textures. We are able to treat an image as a texture and sample from it in the fragment shader. To bind the image as a texture, we load the image outside of the shaders, in our C code. To do this, we first generate a texture object, bind the new texture and copy over the data from the image, which we read in from a bitmap (.BMP) file. We can then access this texture from the fragment shader through a *sampler2D* variable. In our example, we use the Sobel filter for the x coordinate. This is a kernel which can detect vertical lines. For our implementation, we chose to hardcode the kernel values, but these could easily be encoded as another texture or by using the $glGetUniformLocation$ function of OpenGL. The code for the Sobel filter is shown. Applying the sobel filter to a 1920×1080 pixel image, we consistently saw frame-rates in excess of 35 FPS, which is sufficient to meet real-time requirements.

5.3 Neural Network Inferencing

With the recent boom in computational power, machine learning techniques have gained massive popularity and are applied to increasingly diverse domains. Neural networks in specific are applied to a variety of domains with great success. Digital image processing has seen great advancement through the use of neural networks. This has trickled through to embedded systems where machine learning powered image processing algorithms are used for obstacle avoidance and human interaction. However, there has been limited work towards implementing neural networks on GPUs for embedded systems. In addition, this has never been discussed in the context of ARM based embedded clusters. In this section we describe a simple implementation for a dense fully connected neural network. The goal of this is to show that it is possible to implement fairly complicated networks using the restrictive OpenGL ES 2.0 API. In our implementation, all inner products involved in a single layer are handled in parallel by the fragment shader. The input for each layer is prepared and passed in by the draw loop in the C program. The output of each layer is also parsed by the same.

In a neural network, a layer is made up of multiple neurons. Each neuron takes in a vector of the previous layer's output and performs an inner product of this with a weight vector. The result of this inner product is typically passed through an activation function such as a RelU or sigmoid function.

In a single layer of a neural network, each node's output is independent and can be calculated concurrently. Thus, we assign one fragment shader to each node of a layer. For this, each fragment shader needs a way to locate its input values and its weights. For our implementation, we provide both weights and inputs in 1 dimensional arrays to the fragment shader. This is done in the C code by getting a uniform location using $glGetUniformLocation$ which provides a named location which can be accessed by the fragment shader. Then, before calling the rendering pipeline for each layer, we populate the weights, previous layer's output and metadata concerning the size of the current and preceding layer in uniform locations. In the fragment shader, we loop over all outputs of previous layer, multiply these with the appropriate weights and accumulate these in a local variable. This accumulated variable is then output through the red channel of the output color vector.

```
precision mediump float;
uniform float weights[100];
uniform float inputs[10];
uniform int this_layer_width;
uniform int prev_layer_width;

void main() {
        float acc = 0.0;
        int i;
        int neuron_number = int(gl_FragCoord[0]);

        for(i=0; i<prev_layer_width; i++){
                acc += float(weights[neuron_number
                            * prev_layer_width + i])
                      * float(inputs[i]);
        }
        gl_FragColor = vec4(acc/255.0, 0.0, 0.0, 0.0);
}
```

In this example 255 is used to normalise the output of each layer to a value less than 1. This value must be changed depending on the expected maximum output of each layer to prevent clipping. Setting this to a very large value however would lead to loss of precision.

While this paper does not discuss the performance of the system, some considerations regarding performance are fundamental to the final design. Compilation of the vertex and fragment shaders is a fairly expensive task and hence should be minimized. In our implementation, we are able to use a single vertex shader and a single fragment shader, both of which are compiled only once at the very beginning. Further, it is efficient to have a single size for the viewPort since then only a single viewPort of the required dimension is created. For this reason, we chose to create a viewPort of the dimension $largestlayerwidth \times 1$. This would ensure that for each layer, we would have at least as many fragment shader instances as the number of neurons in the layer. Some layers have fewer neurons than the maximum. For these, we avoid placing an if within the fragment shader as this reduces the efficiency on a SIMD processor such as a GPU [14]. Instead, we simply calculate these redundant values and ensure we do not use them when we process the output in the C program. Further, it is essential that we provide a single constant size to the weight and input arrays in the fragment shader. For this, we ensure that the input array is as large as the widest layer, and the weights array is as large as the maximum product of widths of two consecutive layers.

5.4 Usability

In its current form, with the limited interface provided by openGL ES 2.0, it is the view of the authors that any potential speedup gained by using the GPU will be offset by the increased effort required to write a suitable fragment shader and to develop efficient code to communicate with the GPU. To make achieving this speedup less taxing, some form of lightweight framework on top of the existing OpenGL ES 2.0 would be imperative. Further, if a program were able to utilise all 8 GPUs simultaneously, one could expect a significant speedup. This would merit the extra effort required in writing such a program.

Acknowledgments. The authors would like to thank Dr. Kiran D C of Presidency University-Bangalore. His original work towards an embeddable cluster provided the basis for this work. The authors would also like to thank PES University for providing the funding necessary for building PHINEAS.

References

1. 96-core arm supercomputer using the nanopi-fire3. https://climbers.net/sbc/nanopi-fire3-arm-supercomputer/. Accessed 30 Sept 2018
2. Distributed image convolution. https://github.com/arundasan91/MPI---Message-Passing-Interface/blob/master/Image-Scatter-Gather-Tutorial.md
3. Distributed merge sort. https://github.com/racorretjer/Parallel-Merge-Sort-with-MPI/blob/master/merge-mpi.c
4. Hybrid matrix multiplication. http://assets.duet.to/dkl.cs.arizona.edu/teaching/csc522-fall16/examples/hybrid-openmp-mm.c
5. Monte carlo estimation. https://github.com/kiwenlau/MPIPI/blob/master/Montecarlo/mpipi.c
6. NanoPi Fire3. http://wiki.friendlyarm.com/wiki/index.php/NanoPi_Fire3. Accessed 30 Sept 2010
7. NanoPi M1 Plus. http://wiki.friendlyarm.com/wiki/index.php/NanoPi_M1_Plus
8. Neural network training. https://github.com/DT42/neural-network-model-manipulations/blob/master/mnist-nn-data-parallelism.py
9. PINE A64+/PINE A64. https://www.pine64.org/?page_id=1194. Accessed 30 Sept 2010
10. Raspberry Pi 3 model B+ product page. https://www.raspberrypi.org/products/raspberry-pi-3-model-b-plus/. Accessed 30 Sept 2018
11. What is eMMC memory – software support - reliance nitro. https://www.datalight.com/solutions/technologies/emmc/what-is-emmc. Accessed 30 Sept 2018
12. What's a beowulf? http://www.beowulf.org/overview/faq.html
13. M̃unshi, A., G̃insburg, D., Shreiner, D.: OpenGL ES 2.0 Programming Guide. Pearson, London (2009)
14. Fung, W.W., Sham, I., Yuan, G., Aamodt, T.M.: Dynamic warp formation and scheduling for efficient GPU control flow. In: 40th Annual IEEE/ACM International Symposium on Microarchitecture, pp. 407–420 (2007)
15. Kiepert, J.: Creating a Raspberry Pi-based beowulf cluster, pp. 1–17. Boise State University (2013)
16. Sterling, T.L.: Beowulf Cluster Computing with Linux. MIT Press, Cambridge (2002)

MH-QEMU: Memory-State-Aware Fault Injection Platform

Hideyuki Jitsumoto[1(✉)], Yuya Kobayashi[2], Akihiro Nomura[1], and Satoshi Matsuoka[1,3]

[1] Tokyo Institute of Technology, Tokyo, Japan
jitumoto@gsic.titech.ac.jp, nomura.a.ac@m.titech.ac.jp, matsu@acm.org
[2] Digital Media Professionals Inc., Tokyo, Japan
yuya.kobayashi@dmprof.com
[3] RIKEN Center for Computational Science, Kobe, Japan

Abstract. As we move towards higher-density, larger-scale, and lower-power computing hardware, new types of failures are being experienced with increasing frequency. Hardware designed for the post-Moore generation are also bringing about novel resiliency challenges. In order to improve the efficiency of resiliency methods, fault injection plays an important role in understanding how errors affect the OS and application. Memory-state-aware fault injection, in particular, can be used to investigate the memory-related faults caused by using current and future hardware under extreme conditions and assess the costs/benefit trade-off of resiliency methods. We introduce MH-QEMU, a memory-state-aware fault injection platform implemented by extending a virtual machine (VM) to intercepting memory accesses. MH-QEMU supports collecting the physical and virtual addresses of memory accesses and defining appropriate injections condition using the collected information. MH-QEMU incurs a 3.4× overhead, and we demonstrate how row-hammer faults can be injected using MH-QEMU to analyzing the resiliency modified NPB CG's algorithm.

Keywords: Fault injection · Resilience · Virtual machine

1 Introduction

As computing systems increase in scale while simultaneously trending towards higher-density and lower-power hardware, new types of failures are becoming more prevalent and significant. Failures due to Silent Data Corruption (SDC) are examples of such failures that are increasing in frequency. SDC produces incorrect results without raising any errors during an application's execution.

This work was partially supported by JST CREST Grant Numbers JPMJCR1303 and JPMJCR1687, Japan and conducted as research activities of AIST - Tokyo Tech Real World Big-Data Computation Open Innovation Laboratory (RWBC-OIL).

D. Abramson and B. R. de Supinski (Eds.): SCFA 2019, LNCS 11416, pp. 71–85, 2019.
https://doi.org/10.1007/978-3-030-18645-6_5

Furthermore, hardware designed for the post-Moore generation, such as 3D-stacked memories [6,13], and their usage may introduce new failures, such as the degradation of flash memory devices caused by frequent writes to a specific location. In order to improve the efficiency of resiliency strategies, it is necessary to know how errors affect the OS and application in order to apply the appropriate resiliency method based the target and the impact of the resiliency method.

Fault injection is an important technique that is used for investigating the effectiveness of resiliency strategies. However, fault injection on real hardware is very costly since injecting hardware faults typically involves breaking the hardware. Previous work [8,10] has achieved low-cost fault injection by emulating hardware fault with VM's software fault. As a result, some simple faults can be injected easily, such as bit-flip on CPU and memory. Nonetheless, faults that depend on memory state, such as the flash memory degradation mentioned above, is difficult simulated using only the approach described in that work.

We introduce a new fault injection platform, MH-QEMU, which can inject memory-state-aware fault. MH-QEMU is implemented by extending the memory management system of VM and can achieve the following:

- **Injection and flexible description of memory-state-aware fault:** MH-QEMU can emulate various hardware faults affected by memory state and access patterns, such as Row-Hammer [14] on DRAM and the cell degradation on flash memory, by the VMM which can call external modules from VM memory manager.
- **Physical-Virtual placement aware fault injection:** MH-QEMU can modify memory access pattern and its mapping to the physical location by calling external module for each memory access. MH-QEMU also can define the next generation memory module.
- **Supporting analysis of the effects of faults on the system:** For observing the effects of fault on OS and application in the target architecture, it is important to locate the virtual memory address of faults injected by physical memory addresses. MH-QEMU can map such memory addresses and get the information of OS and application without using processes that are executed on a target node.

1.1 Necessity for State-Aware Memory Fault Injection

MH-QEMU aims to simulate SDCs, especially the ones depending on memory access patterns. We focused primarily on the physical location and frequency of access patterns. Examples of this class of corruptions are as follows:

- **Disturbance Error:** As the density of DRAM increases, access to a specific memory cell causes electric interference to surrounding cells, which destroys data.
- **Row-hammer fault in DIMM:** Frequent access to a specific memory row causes fluctuation of the signal voltage of the row-selection line, leading to an increase discharge rate of surrounding rows and loss of data.

- **Deterioration of flash memory:** Memory cells of flash devices are known to become unreliable after a limited number of erase cycles. Either the unreliable cells cannot serve as memory elements or they work as memory elements but cannot provide correct value.

To emulate such hardware-specific errors, it is important to consider the physical properties of the hardware, the electrical and magnetic interactions between multiple components. Flexibility in the descriptions of relationships among components is also required in order to adopt not-well-known error mechanism of emerging hardware architecture, like next-generation memory. Examples of possible new error mechanisms are as follows:

- **Hierarchical usage of different memory architectures:** As a result of the trade-off between cost, speed, and capacity, we often use multiple memory architectures in combination, such as DRAM and NVMe. In such memory systems, memory performance and the error mechanism depend on which physical memory address is accessed.
- **3D structured memory:** Memory architectures achieving high-bandwidth and high-capacity by stacking memory cells vertically to form a 3D structure are currently under active development. As the physical structure is completely different from traditional DIMM, new kinds of disturbance error can occur.

2 Related Work

2.1 Fault Injection to Physical Hardware

Some work simply inject errors by causing physical damage to hardware. Other work inject errors to hardware by neutron beams [19], electromagnetic field [12], heavy-ion beams [9], and so on. Additional hardware has also been employed to inject faults in some manner [1,18]. In these approaches, a fault can be injected easily, but with higher cost: the high cost of procuring additional hardware or causing unrecoverable damage to the system. Furthermore, it is hard to control the location and intensity of the faults being injected.

2.2 Fault Injection by Program Modification

It is possible to inject a code snippet that emulates certain fault behavior into a user program [16]. LLVM-based methods [20] can automatically encode errors to an application without source code modification. These methods can analyze fault effects easily because a user can get detailed information of application processes, such as how the values in memory are used. On the other hands, this method cannot inject hardware specific fault because hardware specific access patterns cannot be determined at program modification time.

2.3 Fault Injection by Virtual Machine (VM)

Error injection to VMM's memory and CPU manager can produce fault on the system executed on VM. In addition, because VMM can dump the state of CPU register and memory value, fault effects can be analyzed in this method without any modification to source code of OS and applications. However, it takes a long time to analyze the effects of injected faults because VMM have to emulate all hardware behavior by software. F-SEFI [8] can inject errors to the logic circuit of CPU, register, and memory modules by this method. D-Cloud [10] is another fault injector by QEMU [4] for hard disk and network controller. D-Cloud can also inject a bit-flip error in memory. Our method, MH-QEMU, also follows this method and the difference from F-SEFI is that MH-QEMU focuses on memory module faults caused by memory state and access pattern. MH-QEMU has APIs that help to analyze memory access behavior, such as a function which maps physical address to virtual address and the reverse in real-time.

3 Design

MH-QEMU is a platform for analyzing memory access patterns of applications and OS and injecting faults depending on the characteristics of the memory modules. The analysis is important for selecting which memory region needs resiliency and what types and levels of resiliency are requested. We assume the following requirements for MH-QEMU's fault injection: (1) no damage to the physical hardware, (2) emulating memory module faults flexibly including those dependent on the memory state and access pattern, and (3) supporting the analysis of the effects of a fault on the OS and application. We choose the VM approach to meet requirement #1 as in previous work (described in Sect. 2.3).

3.1 Emulation of Fault Injection to Memory Module

In order to emulate faults that are dependent on memory state, MH-QEMU gathers memory access pattern, analyses them to create an appropriate fault injection plan, and applies it to target VM memory. To avoid side effects to the target system, the analysis and injection should be done from host OS. To achieve these functionalities, MH-QEMU consists of the following three modules, which is illustrated in Fig. 1:

Memory Mapper of VM to Host (MM). In order to access the VM's memory from the host environment, the MM identifies where the VM's physical memory is located in host's address space and exposes its content to the host. The VM's physical memory is modified when a process on the host OS modifies the exposed place.

Memory Access Handler (MH). User-defined handler functions (MH) can be registered as hooks to load and store accesses to the target VM's memory space. The MH is invoked with trapped memory addresses and arbitrary operations can be executed. Users can collect and analyze memory access patterns and inject faults from MH function.

Fault Injection Scheduler (FS). The FS manages the MM and the MH by following a scenario file that describes the time of fault injection and configurations of MH. To avoid expensive performance losses in the MH execution, FS can enable and disable MH.

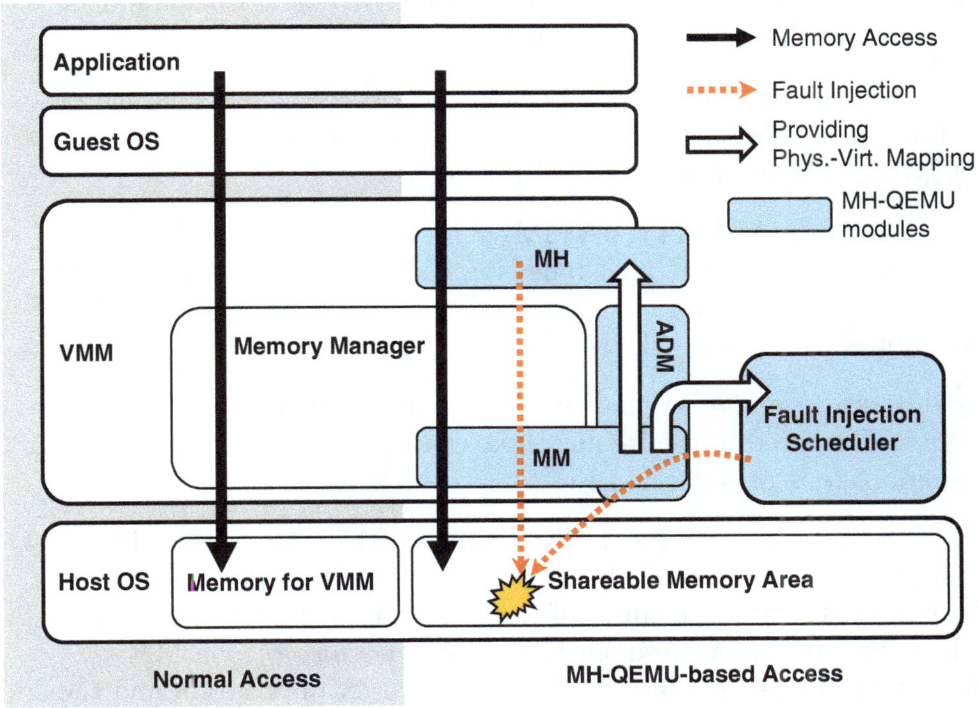

Fig. 1. Overview of MH-QEMU

3.2 Assistance API for Analysis of Fault Effects Inside VM

For detailed analysis and well-controlled injection of faults, MH-QEMU needs to know how the physical memory is used by the guest OS. In addition, MH-QEMU should inject fault based on the memory usage of the guest OS.

Address-Data Mapper (ADM). The ADM retrieves information about the guest OS, such as memory page table and process information. A user can use the ADM from the MH via an API. The ADM can also be called in the configuration script invoked by the target VM for initializing other MH-QEMU modules. In addition, the ADM can dump the process information to storage for off-line data analysis.

3.3 Fault Injection Scenario on MH-QEMU

MH-QEMU invokes the user fault injection code defined by the MH by extended the VMM. For memory-state-aware fault injection, MH-QEMU uses each component in the following manner:

1. User starts a VM extended by MH-QEMU and enables FS.
2. At the appropriate time, the FS invokes the target application in the VM and enables MH using the extended the VMM.
3. When an application process accesses memory, VMM calls the MH with the physical and virtual address of the memory that has been accessed.
4. The MH injects errors and collects various information in cooperation with the ADM.
5. For better performance, the FS disables the MH that will no longer be used since the error is injected only once.

Moreover, the MH should not be used for transient and non-memory-state-aware fault injection since the calling the MH has a high cost. In this case, MH-QEMU can inject fault via the FS as follows:

1. FS suspends the VM via the VMM.
2. FS injects faults via the MM following the user-specified fault injection scenario.
3. FS resumes the VM via the VMM.

To illustrate how the MH can simulate a specific type of fault, we show how a fault can be triggered in the frequently-accessed region of an application's heap. The pseudocode is presented in Fig. 2.

1. MH retrieves the heap memory region by using the ADM with the target application name.
2. MH records (position, counts) of the access to heap region.
3. MH injects an error to frequently-accessed memory bit via MM.
4. MH dumps the process information of the target application and the address where the error was injected. The MH gets the process information from ADM using target application's name.
5. MH reports the injection to the FS.

4 Implementation

MH-QEMU is implemented on top of QEMU 2.3.1. Due to the ADM's implementation, Linux is the only supported guest OS on MH-QEMU. The implementation of each MH-QEMU module (MM, MH, FS, and ADM) is described in the following subsections. API functions for calling other modules from MH module are described in Table 2.

4.1 MM: Memory Mapper

The memory space of a QEMU VM can be mapped into a file in host OS (`-mem-path` option). The MM uses this functionality to enable access to guest OS's memory image from host OS. For performance reason, guest OS's memory space will be mapped to files in `tmpfs`, which is a virtual file system that uses the host system's memory as a data store.

```
memory_access_handler(physaddr, virtaddr){
  range←ADM_get_heep_addr(target_name)
  if (virtaddr is in range){
    count[virtaddr]++
  }
  for(addr←each range){
    if (count[addr] >= threshold){
      records addr
      MM_flipbit(addr)
      ADM_write_processinfo(target_name)
      FS_turnoffMe()
    }
  }
}
```

Fig. 2. Pseudo code of MH

Table 1. Structure of **MHinfo** `target_ulong` is the alias of `unsinged long`

Name	Type	
val	uint64_t	A value which is stored or loaded
dsize	size_t	A size of data which are accessed
gvAddr	target_ulong	Virtual memory address on guest OS
gpAddr	target_ulong	Physical memory address on VM
hvAddr	uintptr_t	Physical memory address on host server
isLoad	bool	True: on load operation, false: on store operation
isBigEndian	bool	GuestVM's endian: true: Big, false: Little

4.2 MH: Memory Access Handler

The MH is implemented as an extension to TCG (Tiny Code Generator), which is a part of QEMU. TCG is a virtualization module for CPU operations. In the TCG layer, all memory access operations are expressed as either `ld`(load) or `st`(store) operations. We added call to the MH (Fig. 3) in the implementation of these operations. The MH is called either before an actual memory store occurs or after an actual load finishes. The MH function takes an argument that is a pointer to the **MHInfo** structure. This structure contains the information on memory access listed in Table 1.

In KVM [15], which utilizes hardware virtualization extensions of CPU to accelerate VM emulation, the TCG is replaced by hardware extensions and MH implementation does not work. However, MH-QEMU can benefit from the accelerated performance in KVM by incorporating other code insertion method. Specifically, memory accesses must be trapped with binary level translator such as Intel Pin [11,17] or dyninst [2].

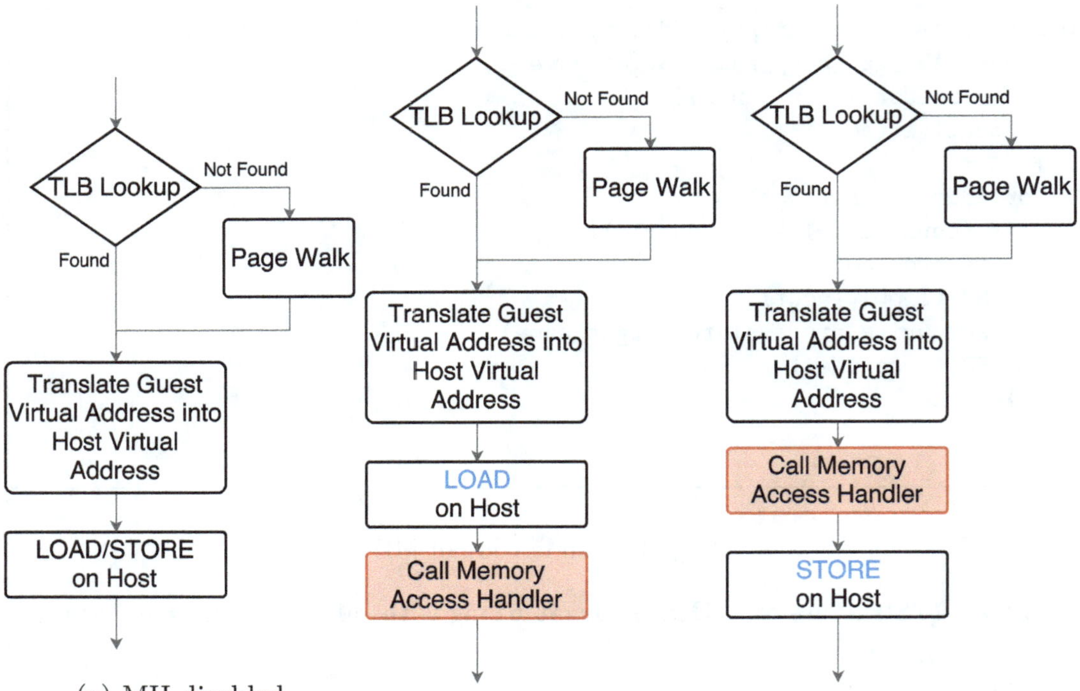

(a) MH disabled

(b) MH enabled, load operation

(c) MH enabled, store operation

Fig. 3. Code generation by TCG

4.3 FS: Fault Injection Scheduler

The FS is a process using extended QMP (QEMU Machine Protocol) and HMP (Human Monitor Protocol). QMP and HMP are protocols for controlling the state of QEMU such as shutdown, making a snapshot, and adding new virtual hardware. We add new entry points to manage MH-QEMU components and the FS calls them to interact with MH-QEMU.

4.4 ADM: Address-Data Mapper

The ADM gets page table and process states from the guest OS. Although this information can be obtained easily in the guest OS, the ADM read them from the outside of VM in order to not modify the memory state of guest OS. The ADM analyzes the VM's memory, via the MM, and gets process information and their page table as follows:

Page Table. The ADM gets the physical address of the kernel page table from the symbol table of the kernel binary by using QEMU and the GDB function. The ADM is able to convert physical memory addresses to virtual memory addresses using this page table if the memory has not been reallocated.

Process Information. Process information in the Linux kernel is managed by a circular list. The ADM can get all process information in the guest OS if

ADM accesses the process information structure of any process. The ADM uses information of the idle process of Linux, since the location of idle process information is stored in a global variable. The ADM can also get process information from the kernel binary with symbols by using QEMU and the GDB function (Fig. 4) in a similar manner as with the page table information described above. The same limitation that memory cannot be reallocated also applies to process information retrieval.

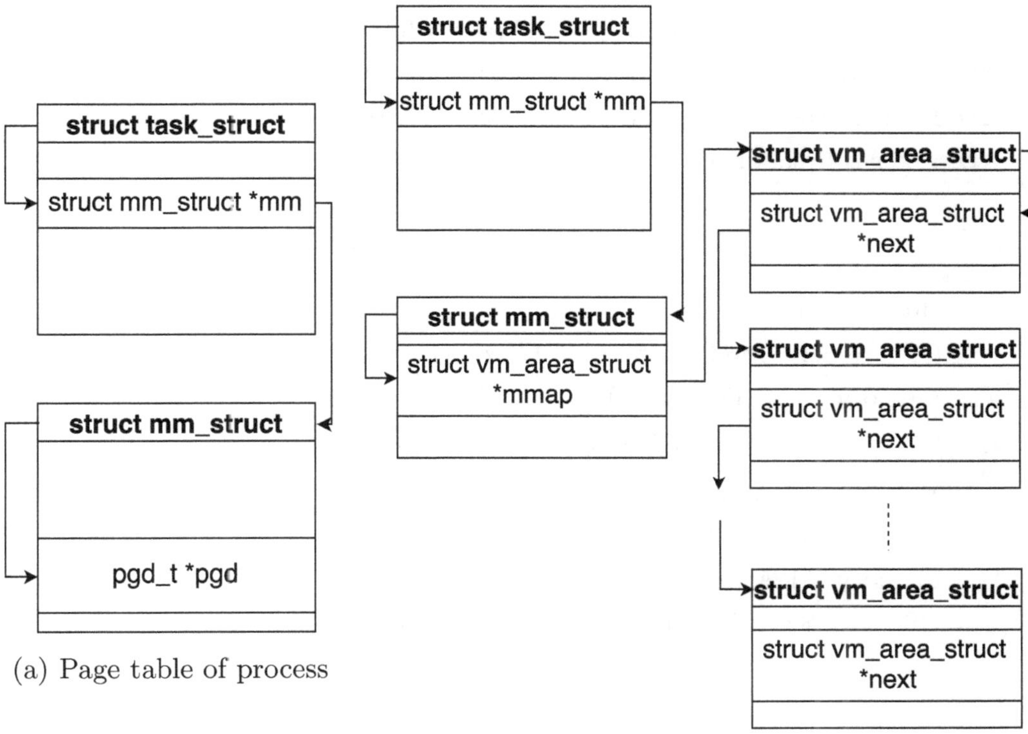

(a) Page table of process

(b) Memory state of process

Fig. 4. Process information of Linux internals: (a) Page table of process, (b) Memory state of process

5 Evaluation and Use Case

We present the overhead of the MH-QEMU platform using the NAS Parallel Benchmark, and we use the CG kernel to illustrate how to use MH-QEMU.

5.1 Evaluation Environment

All evaluations described in this section use a single host server. Eight MH-QEMU VM instances are executed on the server. The specification of the host server and the VM are shown in Table 3.

Table 2. API to MH module from other modules

MM	
MM_set(st, fin, val)	Write value to memory
FS	
FS_turnoff_me()	FS disable MH
ADM	
ADM_write_pagetable(app)	Write a page table to storage
ADM_write_filemapping(app)	Write a file mapping info. to storage
ADM_get_addrange(app, file)	Get addr. range used by app
ADM_conv_virtaddr(physaddr)	Convert virt. addr. to phys. addr
ADM_conv_physaddr(app, virtaddr)	Convert phys. addr. to virt. addr

Table 3. Execution environment

Host Server	
CPU	2 * Intel X5650 (2.67 GHz, 6core/12thread) with VT-x
Memory	ECC DDR4 SDRAM 46 GB
OS	CentOS 7.1 (Linux Kernel 3.10.0)
VM Server (8VM/host)	
CPU	x86_64 Architecture
Memory	512MB
OS	Scientific Linux 7.4 (Linux Kernel 3.10.0)

5.2 Overhead of MH-QEMU Platform

To evaluate the overhead of MH-QEMU platform, we compared the execution time of NAS Parallel Benchmark on native QEMU and on MH-QEMU with empty an MH function. We decomposed the overhead of MH-QEMU to overhead caused by the MM and the overhead caused by MH; the overhead of MM was found to be negligible. Therefore, the overhead of MH-QEMU is almost the same as the overhead of MH. The EP, CG, MG, FT and IS kernels of NAS Parallel Benchmark 3.3.1 were used with the class B problem size. The average execution time of five runs for each kernel is shown in Fig. 5 and Table 4. The overhead of MH-QEMU is normalized to the overhead of naive QEMU. MH-QEMU was up to 3.4 times slower than native QEMU.

5.3 Use Case: Resiliency Analysis of Modified NPB CG

We use NPB CG [3] to demonstrate the usage of MH-QEMU for resiliency analysis. We expect CG already has some algorithm-level resilience to SDC because it uses the inverse power method, an iterative method. In this scenario, we want

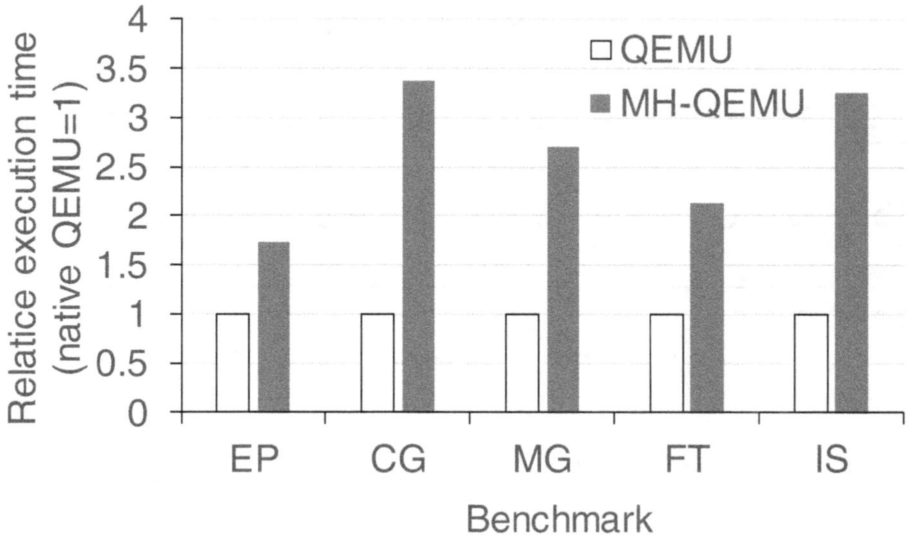

Fig. 5. MH-QEMU overhead toward native QEMU

Table 4. Execution time of QEMU and MH-QEMU (sec.)

	QEMU	MH-QEMU
EP	345.65	596.626
CG	38.676	130.652
MG	98.844	266.458
FT	201.47	428.078
IS	24.38	79.378

to reveal which memory region is weak due to SDC. In the original NPB CG implementation, the number of iteration is fixed as it is intended to be used as a performance benchmark. To evaluate resiliency of the iterative method, we modified NPB CG to continue the iteration until it converges, that is, until the residual becomes less than the 10^{-20}. We inject Row-Hammer faults, which corrupts data in the memory line next to a frequently accessed memory line. We executed 2443 CG runs for this analysis.

Implementation of Row-Hammer MH. The Row-Hammer MH injects the fault as follows:

1. The physical address of each memory access is decomposed into the locations of the physical memory channel, the bank, and the line, following the mapping rule of Intel 82955X-MCH memory structure [5] described in Fig. 6. The MH counts the access for each memory line.
2. If the access counter exceeds the threshold α, the MH determines whether an error is injected with probability λ.

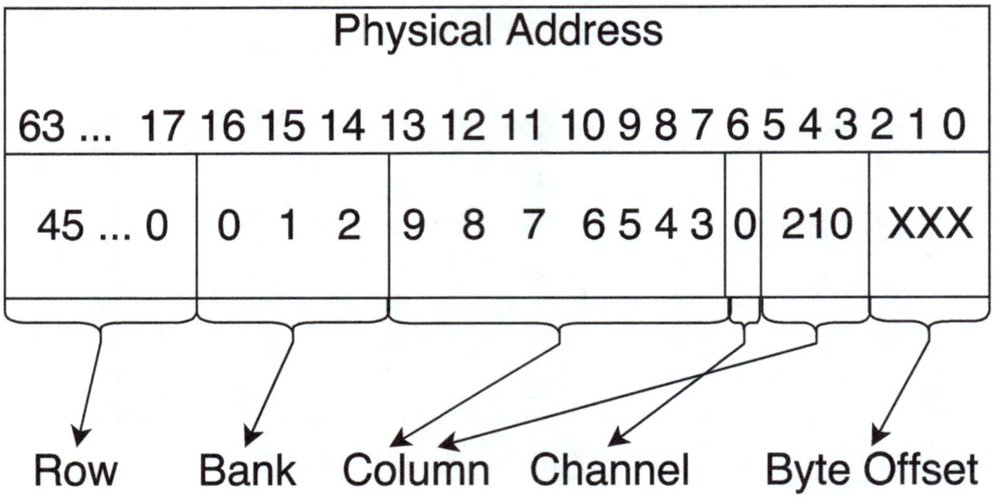

Fig. 6. Mapping rule of Intel 82955X-MCH

3. If the error is to be injected, the MH retrieves the process memory information using the ADM and randomly changes a single bit in the adjacent line of the accessed region to 0. We choose parameters as $\alpha = 1000$ and $\lambda = 5 \times 10^{-10}$

Distribution of Computation Error. A histogram of the computation errors in the results is shown in Fig. 7. The last category labeled as "Abort" represent the number of detectable failed executions. These include when the VM hangs, abnormal termination of the application, and the result containing NaN. Other than such failed execution, all the results fall into one of two categories. We judged that the results with more than 5% error is caused by SDC. In most SDC results, the error is around 166%. It is unknown why they converge to

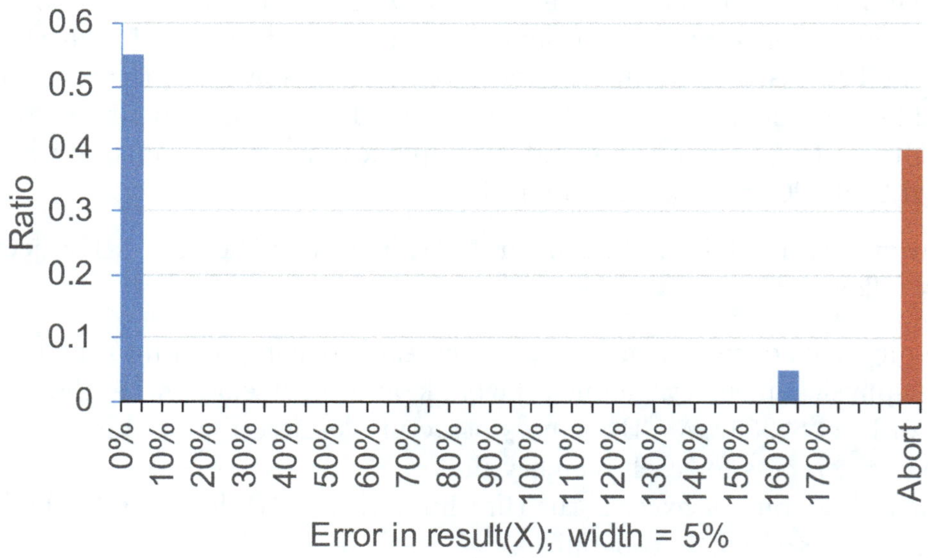

Fig. 7. Histogram of errors

that value as the inverse power method does not have a local solution. On the other hand, 60% of execution return the correct result even after the injection of memory hammer error. This means the CG algorithm has a certain resiliency to SDC.

Relationship Between Fault and Process Memory Region. To investigate the cause of SDC, we select 825 runs at random and mapped the modified data region and execution results, as shown in Fig. 8. The results show that SDC occurs only when the BSS section of CG's binary is modified. The BSS region stores global and static variables with an initial value. Most of the data in BSS region of the CG application kernel are input matrices and intermediate data, modification to which does not lead the application to abnormal termination. In the execution of CG, most of the data are stored in the BSS region, not in the stack. If we analyze the access pattern of each variable to determine its importance, we can specify which variables should be protected to avoid SDCs, without knowledge of CG's algorithm.

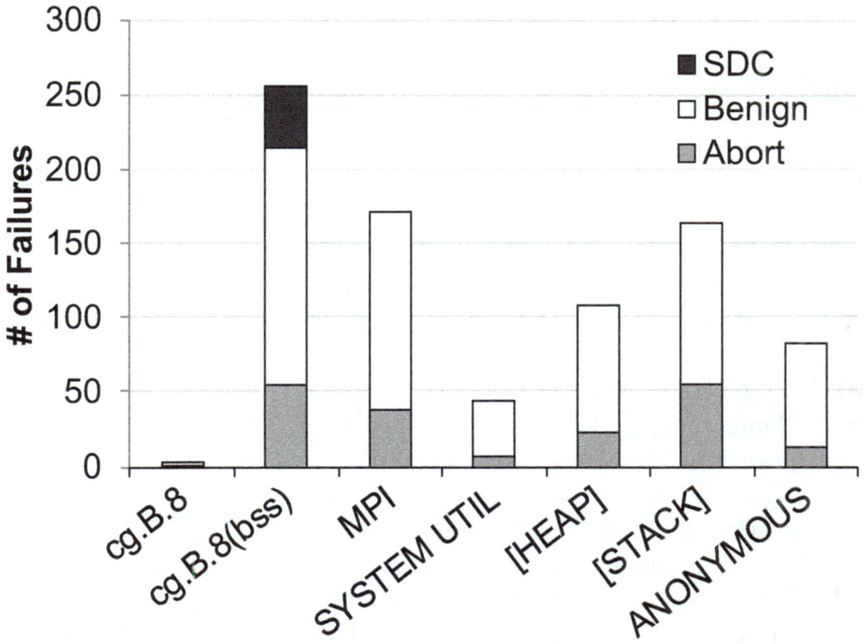

Fig. 8. Effect of error for each memory region in process

6 Conclusion

Brand-new hardware architectures, which has different usage and characteristics from current architectures, are emerging in the post-Moore era. We need fault injectors that can emulate errors in such new architectures in order to develop resiliency methods with the appropriate scope.

We developed MH-QEMU, a fault injector that can generate errors by emulating memory access patterns and the physical structures of memory modules, to accommodate new memory architectures. With MH-QEMU, we can verify resiliency against SDCs brought by architecture-specific properties as well as incidental SDCs.

Currently, the overhead of MH-QEMU is significantly large. It can be reduced by narrowing the memory region that is monitored by the memory handlers. MH-QEMU can also be accelerated by employing hardware-level VM acceleration in KVM when supported by other code insertion methods like Intel Pin [11,17] and dyinst [2].

We are focusing on the the flexibility of fault injection and obtaining the memory location of injected errors at the process level; MH-QEMU does not trace application behavior after fault injection. In future work, we are planning to evaluate application level resiliency for new memory architectures, such as flash memories, 3D stacked memories [6,13], and hierarchical combination with them and DIMMs [7], after enhancement of MH-QEMU for such tracing functionality. If CPU state can be controlled with tools like F-SEFI [8], MH-QEMU approach can be generalized to other types of devices, including network devices and emerging hardware architectures.

References

1. Arlat, J., Crouzet, Y., Laprie, J.C.: Fault injection for dependability validation of fault-tolerant computing systems. In: Nineteenth International Symposium on Fault-Tolerant Computing, FTCS-19. Digest of Papers, pp. 348–355. IEEE (1989)
2. Buck, B., Hollingsworth, J.K.: An API for runtime code patching. Int. J. High Perform. Comput. Appl. **14**(4), 317–329 (2000)
3. Bailey, D.H., et al.: The NAS parallel benchmarks. Int. J. Supercomput. Appl. **5**(3), 63–73 (1991)
4. Bellard, F.: QEMU, a fast and portable dynamic translator. In: USENIX Annual Technical Conference, FREENIX Track, pp. 41–46 (2005)
5. Intel Corporation: Intel 82955x memory controller. https://ark.intel.com/products/27727/Intel-82955X-Memory-Controller
6. Intel Corporation: Intel optane technology. https://www.intel.com/content/www/us/en/architecture-and-technology/intel-optane-technology.html
7. Endo, T.: Realizing out-of-core stencil computations using multi-tier memory hierarchy on GPGPU clusters. In: 2016 IEEE International Conference on Cluster Computing (CLUSTER), pp. 21–29, September 2016. https://doi.org/10.1109/CLUSTER.2016.61
8. Guan, Q., Debardeleben, N., Blanchard, S., Fu, S.: F-sefi: a fine-grained soft error fault injection tool for profiling application vulnerability. In: 2014 IEEE 28th International Parallel and Distributed Processing Symposium, pp. 1245–1254. IEEE (2014)
9. Gunneflo, U., Karlsson, J., Torin, J.: Evaluation of error detection schemes using fault injection by heavy-ion radiation. In: Nineteenth International Symposium on Fault-Tolerant Computing, FTCS-19. Digest of Papers, pp. 340–347. IEEE (1989)
10. Hanawa, T., et al.: Customizing virtual machine with fault injector by integrating with SpecC device model for a software testing environment D-cloud. In: Proceedings - 16th IEEE Pacific Rim International Symposium on Dependable Computing, PRDC 2010, pp. 47–54 (2010). https://doi.org/10.1109/PRDC.2010.37

11. Intel Corporation: Pin - a dynamic binary instrumentation tool. https://software.intel.com/en-us/articles/pin-a-dynamic-binary-instrumentation-tool
12. Karlsson, J., Folkesson, P., Arlat, J., Crouzet, Y., Leber, G., Reisinger, J.: Application of three physical fault injection techniques to the experimental assessment of the mars architecture. Dependable Comput. Fault Tolerant Syst. **10**, 267–288 (1998)
13. Kim, J., Kim, Y.: HBM: memory solution for bandwidth-hungry processors (2014)
14. Kim, Y., et al.: Flipping bits in memory without accessing them: an experimental study of dram disturbance errors. In: ACM SIGARCH Computer Architecture News, vol. 42, pp. 361–372. IEEE Press (2014)
15. Kivity, A., Kamay, Y., Laor, D., Lublin, U., Liguori, A.: KVM: the Linux virtual machine monitor. In: Proceedings of the Linux Symposium, vol. 1, pp. 225–230 (2007)
16. Li, D., Vetter, J.S., Yu, W.: Classifying soft error vulnerabilities in extreme-scale scientific applications using a binary instrumentation tool. In: Proceedings of the International Conference on High Performance Computing, Networking, Storage and Analysis, p. 57. IEEE Computer Society Press (2012)
17. Luk, C.K., et al.: Pin: building customized program analysis tools with dynamic instrumentation. In: Proceedings of the 2005 ACM SIGPLAN Conference on Programming Language Design and Implementation, PLDI 2005, pp. 190–200. ACM, New York (2005). https://doi.org/10.1145/1065010.1065034
18. Madeira, H., Rela, M., Moreira, F., Silva, J.G.: RIFLE: a general purpose pin-level fault injector. In: Echtle, K., Hammer, D., Powell, D. (eds.) EDCC 1994. LNCS, vol. 852, pp. 197–216. Springer, Heidelberg (1994). https://doi.org/10.1007/3-540-58426-9_132
19. Michalak, S.E., et al.: Assessment of the impact of cosmic-ray-induced neutrons on hardware in the roadrunner supercomputer. IEEE Trans. Device Mater. Reliab. **12**(2), 445–454 (2012)
20. Thomas, A., Pattabiraman, K.: LLFI: an intermediate code level fault injector for soft computing applications. In: Workshop on Silicon Errors in Logic System Effects (SELSE) (2013)

Performance Evaluation and Analysis of Linear Algebra Kernels in the Prototype Tianhe-3 Cluster

Xin You, Hailong Yang(✉), Zhongzhi Luan, Yi Liu, and Depei Qian

Sino-German Joint Software Institute, School of Computer Science and Engineering, Beihang University, Beijing 100191, China
{youxin2015,hailong.yang,zhongzhi.luan,yi.liu,depeiq}@buaa.edu.cn

Abstract. As the supercomputing system entering the exascale era, power consumption becomes a major concern in the system design. Among all the novel techniques for reducing power consumption, ARM architecture is gaining popularity in the HPC community due to its low power footprint and high energy efficiency. As one of the initiatives for addressing the exascale challenges in China, Tianhe-3 supercomputer has adopted the technology roadmap of using the many-core ARM architecture with home-built phytium-2000+ and matrix-2000+ processors. In this paper, we evaluate several linear algebra kernels such as matrix-matrix multiplication, matrix-vector multiplication and triangular solver with both sparse and dense datasets. These linear algebra kernels are good performance indicators of the prototype Tianhe-3 cluster. Comprehensive analysis is performed using roofline model to identify the directions for performance optimization from both hardware and software perspectives. In addition, we compare the performance of phytium-2000+ and matrix-2000+ with widely used KNL processor. We believe this paper provides valuable experiences and insights as work-in-progress towards exascale for the HPC community.

Keywords: Exascale · Performance evaluation and analysis · Roofline model · Tianhe-3 cluster

1 Introduction

Evolving the supercomputing towards the exascale still remains an open challenge for the entire HPC community. Although the technical roadmap varies within the community, there is a consensus that the power consumption must be constrained for the next generation supercomputer to be practically sustainable. For instance, the US Department of Energy Exascale Initiative Steering Committee establishes a 20 MW power budget for the exascale supercomputer [27]. Among the innovative approaches that have been exploited to achieve such power efficiency at large scale, the ARM architecture has drawn the attention of the

D. Abramson and B. R. de Supinski (Eds.): SCFA 2019, LNCS 11416, pp. 86–105, 2019.
https://doi.org/10.1007/978-3-030-18645-6_6

HPC community for its merit of lower power consumption yet competitive performance. Benchmarks have been evaluated to show the effectiveness of using ARM based processors for scientific applications under power constraint [20,25,26]. In addition, experimental clusters have been built with scientific benchmarks evaluated to demonstrate the feasibility of using ARM based processors for constructing supercomputers [23,24]. Therefore, ARM based solutions have already shown their potential to achieve the power efficiency towards exascale.

Among the exascale initiatives in China, Tianhe-3 has adopted the ARM based many-core architecture roadmap using home built phytium and matrix processors. Especially, matrix-2000 processor has already demonstrated its capability for performance acceleration on the previous generation supercomputer Tianhe-2A [9]. Recently, the supercomputing team for Tianhe-3 has opened a prototype Tianhe-3 cluster built upon phytium-2000+ (FTP) and matrix-2000+ (MTP) processors to the public for performance evaluation. This paper takes this rare opportunity to perform comprehensive evaluation of the prototype Tianhe-3 cluster and report the evaluation results as work-in-progress for the HPC community towards exascale.

During the performance evaluation, we use several important linear algebra kernels such as matrix-matrix multiplication, matrix-vector multiplication and triangular solver with both dense and sparse datasets. These linear algebra kernels serve as the fundamental building blocks not only for scientific applications such as computational fluid dynamics (CFD) [12] and molecular dynamics (MD) [22], but also for emerging applications such as graph computing [14] and deep neural networks [13]. We also compare the performance of FTP and MTP processors with widely adopted Intel KNL processor [28] quantitatively. We hope the evaluation results and roofline model analysis from this paper serve in two folds. On one hand, it reveals the architecture designs that are important to achieve the exascale performance with limited power budget for hardware architects. On the other hand, it highlights the factors that software developer should take into consideration for writing efficient code on the near future exascale supercomputers.

Specifically, this paper makes the following contributions:

- We provide a comprehensive performance evaluation of the prototype Tianhe-3 cluster that uses ARMv8-based many-core FTP and MTP processors with important linear algebra kernels.
- We compare the performance of the FTP and MTP processors with their industry counterpart Intel KNL many-core processor, which reveals the strengths and weaknesses among these architecture designs.
- We build roofline models for FTP, MTP and KNL processors to understand the limiting factors that impact the performance of these linear algebra kernels and highlight the directions for performance optimization.

The remainder of this paper is organized as follows. In Sect. 2, we describe the background of our evaluation, including the mathematics of the linear algebra kernels as well as the specifications of the prototype Tianhe-3 cluster. Section 3 presents the evaluation results on both single node FTP and MTP processor as well as at cluster scale. In addition, we compare the performance results on both FTP and MTP processors with Intel KNL processor. In Sect. 4, we build the roofline models to better understand the evaluation results and identify the directions for performance optimization. The related work is illustrated in Sect. 5. We conclude this paper in Sect. 6.

2 Background

2.1 Linear Algebra Kernels

Matrix-Matrix Multiplication. GEMM (General Matrix-Matrix Multiplication) is the most commonly used linear algebra kernel in scientific applications. As shown in Fig. 1(a), the GEMM routine can be described as Eq. 1, where A, B and C are Matrices with dimensions $(n \times k)$, $(k \times m)$ and $(n \times m)$, α and β are scalars. As GEMM can reach high arithmetic intensity to stress the processor when matrix size is large enough, it is an ideal benchmark kernel to evaluate the performance of a particular processor. On the other hand, GEMM is also a key kernel for widely used deep neural networks such as AlexNet [13] and ResNet [30]. The performance of GEMM reflects how well these deep neural networks run on the prototype Tianhe-3 cluster.

$$C = \alpha AB + \beta C \tag{1}$$

Matrix-Vector Multiplication. Matrix-vector multiplication can be defined as Eq. 2, where A is a $(n \times m)$ matrix, x and y are vectors of n rows and α, β are scalars. For applications that use sparse matrix, sparse matrix-vector multiplication (SpMV) is proposed to avoid storing and computing redundant zero values to reduce both storage and computation complexity. The computation of SpMV is shown in Fig. 1(b), where matrix A is sparse matrix, x and y vectors are dense. Different storage forms are proposed with different SpMV algorithms, such as CSR [32], CSR5 [15] and ELLPACK [16]. There are several attributes that can describe the property of a sparse matrix, including matrix size n, the number of non-zero values nnz and sparsity nnz/n. The computation challenge of SpMV is the high memory bandwidth demand due to its poor data locality. Therefore, we choose SpMV as a memory-bound kernel to evaluate the prototype Tianhe-3 cluster.

$$y = \alpha Ax + \beta y \tag{2}$$

Triangular Solver. The math form of TRSV (Triangular Solver) is defined as Eq. 3, where L is the triangular matrix and x is the unknown vector to be solved, which has the same shape as the given vector b. Figure 1(c) shows the computation of TRSV where matrix L is non-unit lower triangular matrix. In general, TRSV is less computation intensive as GEMM. However, the computation of TRSV involves strong data dependency, which becomes more difficult to solve when scaling up to multiple computing nodes. Specifically, TRSV stresses the computation of a single node as well as the interconnect across multiple nodes.

$$Lx = b \tag{3}$$

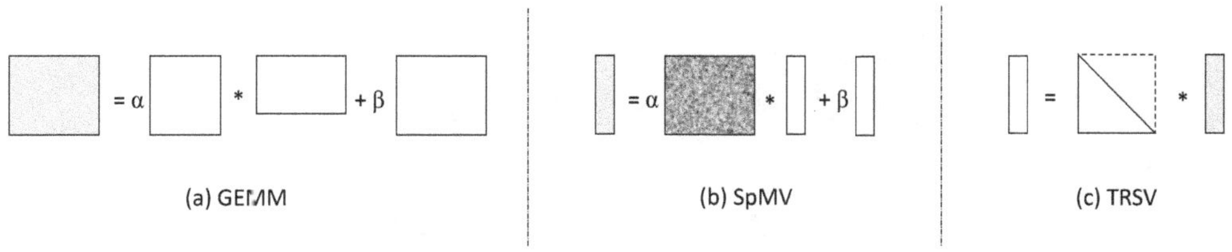

Fig. 1. The computation illustration of linear algebra kernels: (a) GEMM (b) SpMV (c) TRSV. The gray rectangle is the output of the kernel, the white rectangle is dense matrix/vector and the rest is sparse matrix.

2.2 Prototype Tianhe-3 Cluster

The prototype Tianhe-3 cluster is located in Tianjin, China. However, due to the confidentiality agreement, very few technical details about Phytium FT-2000+ (FTP) and MT-2000+ (MTP) processors are released to us. Based on the public reports [9,10,35] as well as the information told by the managing staffs, FTP contains 64 ARMv8 cores, which are organized into eight panels as shown in Fig. 2(a). Each core can run up to 2.4 GHz with the entire processor offering around 614.4Gflops double-precision peak performance and consuming 100 Watts at maximum. Whereas for MTP, it contains 128 ARMv8 cores, which are organized into 4 supernodes as shown in Fig. 2(b). Each core can run up to 2.0 GHz with the entire processor offering around 4.096Tflops double-precision peak performance and consuming 240 W.

During our evaluation, however, the core resources in the prototype cluster are deliberately split at the granularity of 32 cores (one computing node) for both FTP and MTP processors. The reason is that the supercomputing center can offer more computing nodes to serve the demanding evaluation requests in the prototype cluster. The computing nodes are managed and assigned by the batch scheduling system. The user can request the computing node to be allocated as either a FTP node with 32 cores and 64 GB memory or MTP node with 32 core and 16 GB memory. Both FTP and MTP nodes are running Kylin 4.0-1a OS with kernel v4.4.0.

The interconnect in the prototype cluster is built by the National University of Defense Technology (NUDT) that provides 200 Gbps bi-directional bandwidth. The distributed storage nodes are managed by Lustre that provides the shared file system for the prototype cluster. For the compile environment, both GCC v4.9.3 and v4.9.1 as well as a customized MPICH v3.2.1 are supported. The prototype cluster also supports widely used libraries such as BLAS and

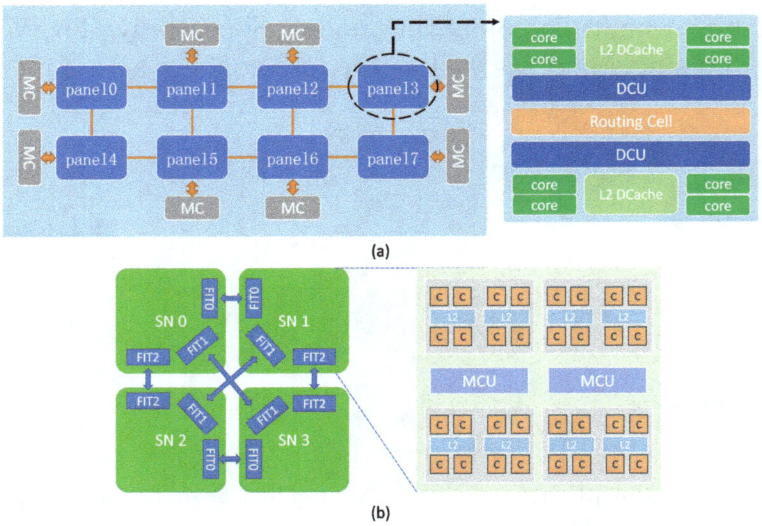

Fig. 2. The architecture of (a) FT-2000+ processor and (b) MT-2000+ processor.

Boost. Therefore, it is very smooth for most of the scientific applications to be ported to run on the prototype cluster. The available hardware and software specifications of the prototype cluster are listed in Table 1.

Table 1. The available hardware and software specifications of the prototype cluster.

Specifications		FT-2000+	MT-2000+
Hardware	Nodes	128	512
	Cores in a node	32	32
	Frequency	2.4 GHz	2.0 GHz
	Memory	64 GB	16 GB
	Interconnect bandwidth	200 Gbps	
Software	OS	Kylin 4.0-1a OS with kernel v4.4.0	
	File system	Lustre	
	MPI	MPICH v3.2.1	
	Compiler	GCC v4.9.1/v4.9.3	
	Supported libraries	Boost, BLAS, OpenBLAS, Scalapack, etc.	

3 Evaluation

3.1 Experimental Setup

To evaluate the linear algebra kernels in the prototype cluster, we choose the widely used library implementations whenever possible. In addition, we also choose open source implementations that are highly rated in the literature. We explicitly choose the dense and sparse implementations since they use different optimization strategies and stress different aspects of the processor. The selection of linear algebra kernels is detailed in Table 2.

Table 2. Linear algebra kernels under evaluation.

Platforms	FTP			MTP			KNL		
Kernels	GEMM	TRSV	SpMV	GEMM	TRSV	SpMV	GEMM	TRSV	SpMV
Openblas [34]	✓	✓		✓	✓				
Intel MKL [31]							✓	✓	✓
Scalapack [2]	✓	✓	✓	✓	✓	✓			
CSR [32]			✓			✓			
distributedSpMV [11]			✓			✓			

For the datasets, we generate the dense square matrices ($N \times N$) with random double-precision values. We scale the dense matrices from $N = 32$ to $N = 6400$ to see how they affect the processor performance at scale. For the sparse matrices, we use the 20 square matrices from the popular Florida Sparse Matrix Collection [6]. These sparse matrices are representative of a wide variety of application domains such as graphic computing and scientific application. The unique characteristics of each sparse matrix are listed in Table 3.

We evaluate the linear algebra kernels on a single node as well as across multiple nodes with both FTP and MTP processors. For both FTP and MTP processors, we use up to 64 nodes (2048 cores) at the largest scale that we can apply. For comparison, we also evaluate the Intel KNL many-core processor Xeon Phi 7210 that contains 64 cores with each running at 1.3 GHz. We use the MKL libraries on KNL that are highly optimized for the linear algebra kernels on Intel architecture. We use the flat mode of the hybrid memories on KNL and allocate the data on the High Bandwidth Memory (HBM), which provides higher bandwidth for memory accesses and thus better performance. OpenMP and MPI are used as the parallel execution models during the evaluation.

3.2 Performance Comparison on Singe Node

The evaluation of each processor using specific kernel implementation is shown in Table 2. To measure the performance of a single node, we utilize all the cores to run the kernels on each particular processor. Specifically, we run 32 threads on FTP and MTP node respectively, whereas 64 threads on KNL. Figure 3 shows the box plot of the single node performance when running GEMM, TRSV and SpMV on FTP, MTP and KNL respectively. We can see that KNL achieves the best average performance across all three kernels. For dense kernels such as GEMM, KNL achieves 6.8× and 14.0× performance speedup compared to FTP and MTP respectively. The large performance gap of GEMM on KNL compared to FTP

Table 3. The sparse matrix datasets under evaluation.

Matrix shape	Matrix	row×col	nnz	nnz/row
	G24	2K × 2K	39.9K	19.9
	windtunnel_evap2d	8K × 8K	109K	13
	vsp_c-30_data_data	11K × 11K	124K	11
	TEM152078	15K × 15K	6.5M	42
	EAT_RS	23K × 23K	325K	14
	epb2	25K × 25K	175K	7
	cit−HepTh	27K × 27K	352K	13
	invextr1_new	30K × 30K	1.8M	59
	ship_001	35K × 35K	3.9M	112
	onetone1	36K × 36K	335K	9
	bcsstk32	44K × 44K	2.0M	45
	venkat01	62K × 62K	1.7M	28
	nd24k	72K × 72K	28.7M	398
	ifiss_mat	96K × 96K	3.6M	37
	barrier2−10	115K × 115K	2.1M	18
	torso1	116K × 116K	8.5M	73
	scircuit	171K × 171K	959K	6
	offshore	259K × 259K	4.2M	16
	ASIC_680ks	682K × 682K	1.7M	2.5
	thermal2	1.2M × 1.2M	8.6M	7

and MTP is due to the limited core count assigned for each computing node in the prototype Tianhe-3 cluster. For instance, on both FTP and MTP computing nodes, there are only 32 cores. Whereas on KNL, there are 64 cores available. Large core count clearly gives an advantage from the performance perspective. It is also noticed from Fig. 3(a) and (b), FTP achieves better performance than MTP for the dense kernels (GEMM and TRSV). This is because, although FTP and MTP node contain the same core count (e.g., 32), the cores in FTP run at higher frequency (e.g., 2.4 GHz) than the cores (e.g., 2.0 GHz) on MTP.

For the sparse kernel such as SpMV, the performance gap of FTP and MTP processor compared to KNL becomes even larger as shown in Fig. 3(c). The average performance of SpMV on KNL is 15.4× and 16.6× better than on FTP and MTP respectively. It is well understood that the performance of SpMV is

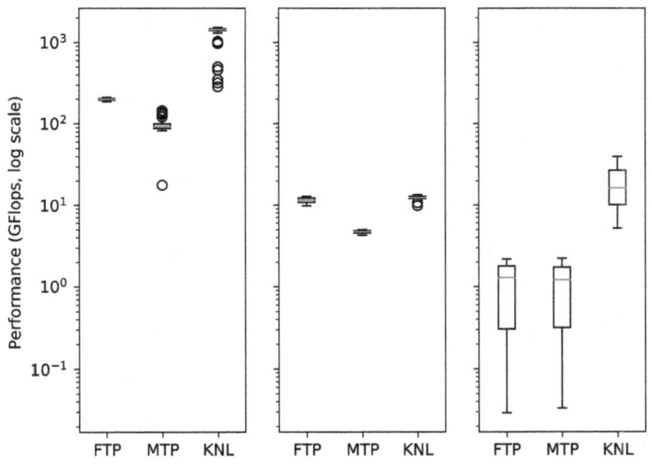

Fig. 3. The performance comparison among FTP, MTP and KNL running linear algebra kernels of (a) GEMM, (b) TRSV and (c) SpMV.

bounded by the memory bandwidth due to its nature of poor data locality. Therefore, the core count as well as the core frequency should not be the dominating factors for the performance disparity among the processors. We believe the performance advantage of KNL can be partially attributed to the high bandwidth memory (HBM) integrated into the processor, which provides much higher memory bandwidth than FTP and MTP that use the traditional DRAM. In addition, the MKL provides highly optimized SpMV implementation that leverages the powerful vectorization capability of KNL through AVX512 instructions, which achieves tremendous speedup of SpMV. In contrast, the capability of vectorization on FTP and MTP is quite limited compared to KNL. Recent work [5] even claims vectorization of SpMV on FTP provides no performance benefit if not slow down. In general, the low memory bandwidth as well as the limited vectorization of FTP and MTP hurt their ability to deliver comparable performance of SpMV to their counterpart KNL.

3.3 Scalability Comparison

In order to compare the performance scalability of the kernels on different processors, we scale the kernel execution on both a single node and across multiple nodes. For single node scalability, we run each kernel from 1 to 32 threads on FTP and MTP, whereas from 1 to 64 threads on KNL. The speedup of each kernel is compared to the single thread execution. Figure 4(a) shows the single node scalability of GEMM on these three processors. We can see that GEMM reaches good scalability on a single node with maximum speedup of 23.8× on FTP, 20.3× on MTP and 42.7× on KNL. The huge speedup achieved by GEMM when scaling on KNL can be attributed to the large core count compared to FTP and MTP. For TRSV, the scalability on KNL starts to drop beyond 32 threads. The maximum speedup achieved on FTP, MTP and KNL is 6.9×, 3.3× and 3.8× respectively as shown in Fig. 4(b). However, the absolute performance on

KNL is always better than FTP and MTP at all scales. For SpMV, the scalability of FTP and MTP is extremely poor. The maximum speedup of SpMV is 2.4× and 2.7× on FTP and MTP respectively when utilizing half of the cores as shown in Fig. 4(c). In contrast, KNL scales well and reaches maximum speedup of 30.1× when all cores are fully utilized. Since SpMV is memory bounded, the good scalability is primarily due to the high bandwidth memory (HBM) on KNL that offers 400+ GB/s bandwidth compared to FTP and MTP that use DRAM for quite limited bandwidth.

For the scalability across multiple nodes, we run each kernel from 1 to 64 computing nodes with each node fully utilized (e.g., running 32 threads). We do not include the results of multiple KNL nodes since we only have one KNL node available. The speedup of each kernel is compared to the single node execution. Figure 5(a) shows that the performance speedup of GEMM starts to drop on FTP when the number of nodes scales beyond 32. Therefore, MTP has better scalability when running GEMM compared to FTP. However, the absolute performance of GEMM is, on the contrary, better on FTP even scaling beyond 32 nodes. For TRSV shown in Fig. 5(b), the performance speedup starts to drop on both FTP and MTP processor when the number of nodes scales beyond 32. The maximum speedup is 3.5× and 5.7× when running on 32 nodes of FTP and MTP respectively. For SpMV, the maximum performance speedup is 1.8× on FTP with 8 nodes and 5.8× on MTP with 32 nodes as shown in Fig. 5(c). The scalability of FTP is much worse than MTP, where the performance speedup starts to drop beyond eight nodes.

4 Discussion

4.1 Building the Roofline Model

To better understand the evaluation results on FTP, MTP as well as KNL, we build the Roofline Model [33] to investigate the strengths and weaknesses of each processor architecture. The advantage of the roofline model is that it establishes a quantitative relationship among floating-point performance, operational intensity and memory performance using a 2D graph, which captures the intrinsic characteristics of hardware and software designs. Using the roofline model, it is easy to reveal the performance upper bound on each processor. The *roof* in the roofline model indicates the peak performance of the processor, whereas the *slope* indicates the peak memory bandwidth. The x axis measures the operational intensity of the program under evaluation, and the y axis indicates the attainable performance (GFlops). Depending on whether the column of the operational intensity hits the flat part of the roof, we can easily identify whether the program under evaluation is compute-bound or memory-bound.

To obtain the peak floating-point performance of FTP and MTP processors, we scale down the original processor specifications [9, 10, 35] proportional to the core count of a compute node in the prototype cluster. For KNL, we provide the theoretical peak floating-point performance from processor specifications. To

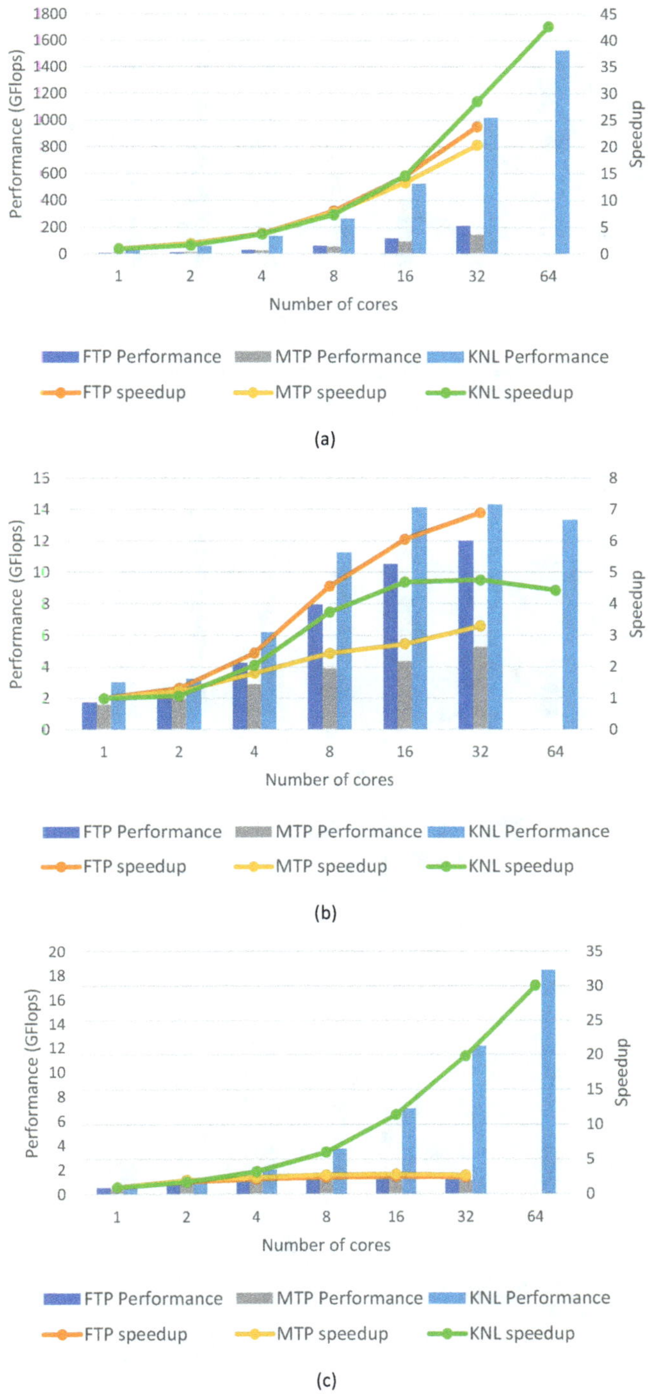

Fig. 4. Scalability of (a) GEMM, (b) TRSV and (c) SpMV on a single node.

obtain the peak memory bandwidth, we use *STREAM* benchmark [17] to measure the three processors directly. We also add multiple ceilings to the roofline model by using different optimizations. For instance, we add one memory ceiling by using the memory affinity optimization and several compute ceilings by using thread-level parallelism (TLP), instruction-level parallelism (ILP) as well

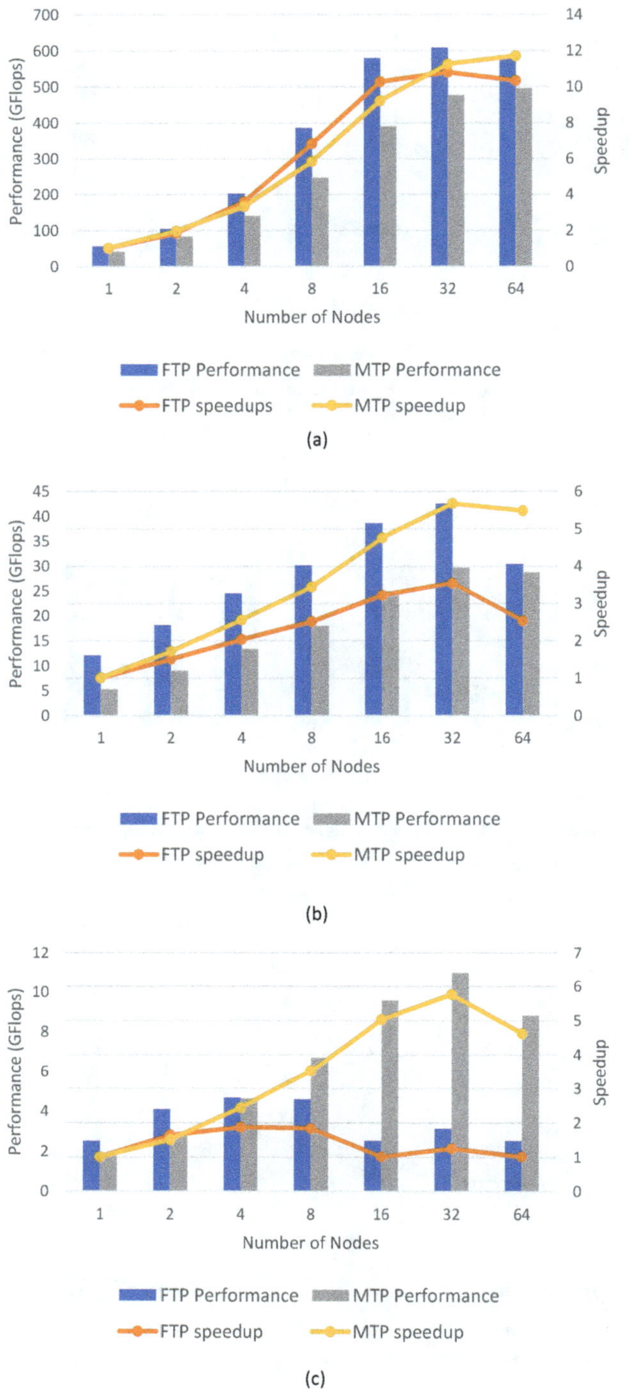

Fig. 5. Scalability of (a) GEMM, (b) TRSV and (c) SpMV across multiple nodes.

as SIMD instructions. These ceilings in the roofline model are intuitive to guide the directions for performance optimization.

$$OperationalIntensity = Flops/Bytes \tag{4}$$

Table 4. The formulas [21] for calculating operational intensity of evaluated kernels, where n is the size of matrix, nnz is the number of non-zero values in sparse matrix.

Kernel	Flops	Data movement (bytes)	Operational intensity
GEMM	$2n^3$	$4n^2 * 8$	$n/16$
TRSV	n^2	$n(n+1)/2+n$	$2n/(n+3)$
SpMV	$2nnz$	$4*(n+1+nnz)+8*(2n+nnz)$	$nnz/(6n+2+10nnz)$

To measure the operational intensity, we calculate the flops and data movements of each kernel based on the given input. Generally, the operational intensity is calculated as shown in Eq. 4, where *Flops* is the number of floating point operations and *Bytes* are the total bytes of data movements from DRAM. The formulas for calculating *Flops*, *Bytes* and *OperationalIntensity* for the evaluated kernels are shown in Table 4. Specifically, *Data Movement* differs when using different implementations, therefore we use the theoretical minimal of *Data Movement*, assuming all data can be fully reused. The results shown in Figs. 6, 7 and 8 are evaluated against different kernels with different inputs running on each of the three processors.

4.2 Insights for Software Optimization

As shown in Fig. 6, the kernel GEMM achieves the highest operational intensity across all three kernel, which is consistent with its nature of high intensity of arithmetic operations. It is also clear that GEMM is compute-bound on FTP. Since GEMM is usually one of the highly optimized kernels in modern linear algebra libraries, it is quite close to the theoretical ceiling of FTP especially when the matrix size scales. Therefore, there is not too much opportunity from

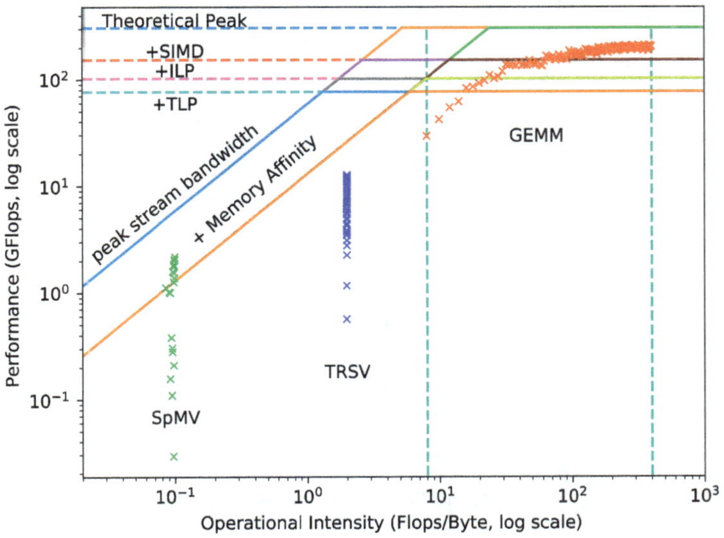

Fig. 6. The roofline model of FTP.

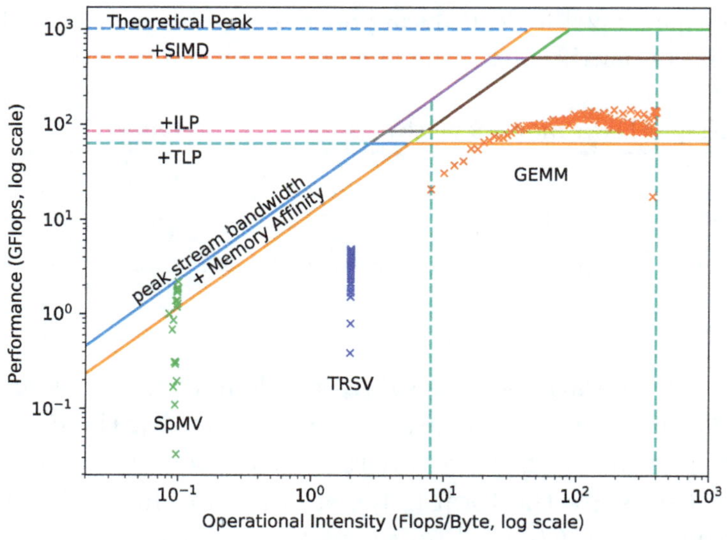

Fig. 7. The roofline model of MTP.

the software perspective for future performance optimization unless more cores are added or the frequency of each core is increased. However, developers still need to consider the memory affinity when the matrix size is small. Otherwise, the performance of GEMM could be bounded by the memory indicated by the lower memory ceiling in Fig. 6.

TRSV and SpMV show much lower operational intensity on FTP compared to GEMM. In addition, the performance of both TRSV and SpMV is memory bounded as shown in Fig. 6. Especially for SpMV, the operational intensity is the lowest among all three kernels due to its poor data locality. Different from GEMM where the operational intensity covers a wide range as the matrix size

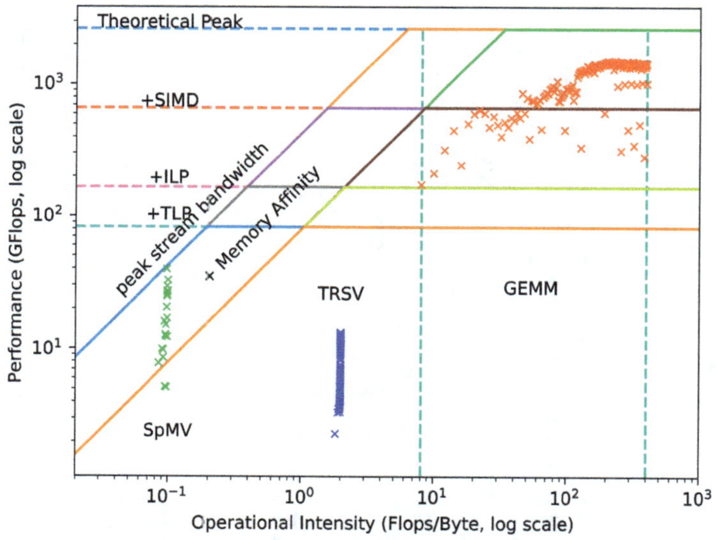

Fig. 8. The roofline model of KNL.

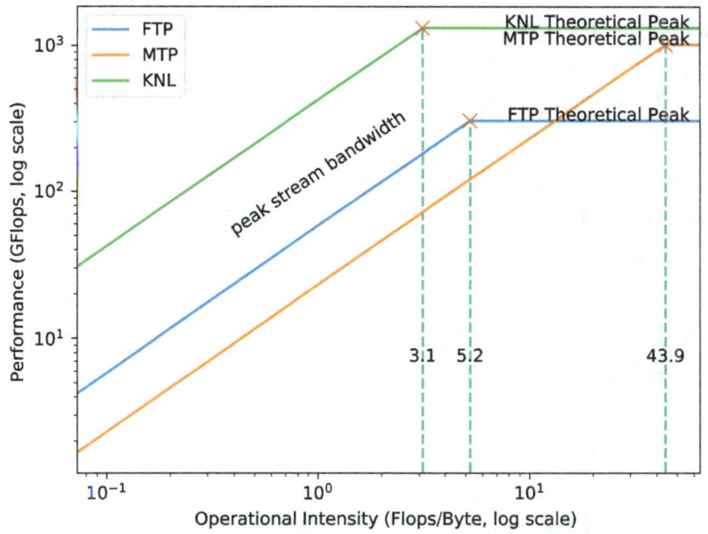

Fig. 9. The performance comparison of different processors using roofline model.

scales, the operational intensity of both TRSV and SpMV converges when the matrix size is large enough. As shown in Fig. 6, the performance of both TRSV and SpMV is still bounded by the lower memory ceiling (e.g., memory affinity). Therefore, using the memory node close to the computation could benefit the performance of both TRSV and SpMV on FTP.

Note that memory affinity is an important factor to achieve better performance on FTP. As shown in Fig. 2(a), the cores in FTP are organized into several panels and each panel has a local memory node attached. Therefore, the developers should pay special attention to the memory affinity when writing applications on FTP in case of bounding by the lower memory ceiling. Another interesting thing we can notice from Fig. 6 is that the computing ceilings (e.g., TLP, ILP and SIMD) are quite near to each other, which means applying a single optimization on FTP could not increase the performance significantly. However, there is still a large performance space between the ceiling of TLP and theoretical peak. Therefore, it still worths the effort to optimize the applications from computation aspect on FTP.

Although the performance trends of TRSV and SpMV on MTP are similar (e.g., memory-bound) to FTP, the behavior of GEMM is somehow different as shown in Fig. 7. Half of the cases, the performance of GEMM is memory-bound. When the operational intensity is high enough, it becomes compute-bound. However, we notice when GEMM becomes compute-bound, its performance starts to drop. The reason for this interesting trend of GEMM can be explained that when the operational intensity is low (e.g., small matrix size), the performance is bounded by the limited memory bandwidth (e.g., 16 GB on MTP compared to 64GB on FTP). As the operational intensity increases, the insufficient computing capacity (e.g., 2.0 GHz on MTP compared to 2.4 GHz on FTP) prevents GEMM from achieving higher performance.

We also notice that the performance space between the ceiling of TPL and the theoretical peak is quite large in Fig. 7. The SIMD instructions are wider on MTP than FTP. The wider SIMD instructions on MTP indicate a large performance opportunity if the application can vectorize its computation on MTP. The computation of GEMM itself fits well for vectorization. Therefore, how to leverage the SIMD instructions on MTP should be the direction for further performance optimization of GEMM from the software perspective.

The computing ceilings are quite far from each other as shown in Fig. 8. The similar trend is also observed with memory ceilings. This indicates performance optimizations are indispensable for applications to run efficiently on KNL, especially for TRSV, which achieves even worse performance than SpMV in many cases. Two potential directions for improving the performance of TRSV on KNL are *(1)* breaking the memory ceiling by leveraging the memory affinity, and *(2)* breaking the TLP ceiling by exposing sufficient parallelism. To break the memory ceiling, exploiting the unique high bandwidth memory (HBM) on KNL should benefit the performance by providing higher memory bandwidth. Whereas to break the ILP ceiling, loop unrolling and reordering should be applied to increase the instruction parallelism.

4.3 Insights for Hardware Optimization

Obviously shown in Fig. 9, KNL delivers the highest performance compared to FTP and MTP due to its large number of cores and wider SIMD units. Therefore, to approach exascale, sufficient core count and powerful vectorization is essential for the future architecture improvement on both FTP and MTP. Another interesting observation is that the ridge point of KNL is more left than FTP and MTP in the roofline model. The ridge point indicates the minimum operational intensity required to achieve the peak performance. Therefore, the more left the ridge point is, the fewer restrictions there are for application to reach the peak performance on the processor. For instance, the ridge points for KNL, FTP and MTP are 3.1, 5.2 and 43.9 Flops/Byte respectively, which means MTP is the most difficult processor for developers and compiler writers to produce high-performance programs. To improve the productivity on the future exascale supercomputer, reducing the operational intensity of both FTP and MTP benefits from all types of software optimizations. In addition, the diagonal line of KNL is also much higher than FTP and MTP, which means KNL provides much higher memory bandwidth than the other two processors. This can be attributed to the adoption of high bandwidth memory (HBM) in KNL that application can leverage by expressing the memory affinity. Integrating the traditional DRAM with novel memory technologies such as HBM could be another hardware optimization for FTP and MTP in order to eliminate the potential memory bound.

5 Related Work

5.1 Performance Optimization of Linear Algebra Kernels

Linear Algebra Kernels such as GEMM, TRSV and SpMV are widely used in scientific computing and machine learning. Many optimization works are focused on these Linear Algebra Kernels to gain full advantage of specific architectures. For dense matrix multiplication and solvers, BLAS gives an overall interface for all kinds of linear algebra kernels. OpenBLAS [34] is an open source implementation of BLAS interface with optimization of thread parallelization and blocking techniques. Scalapack [2] is also available in Tianhe-3 prototype cluster for scaling the BLAS interface to the distributed cluster. Intel Math Kernel Library (MKL) [31] is specially designed for x86 processors and by using parallelization, vectorization, blocking and other specified optimizing techniques, it reaches a notable performance gain than many other open source libraries.

In the case of sparse matrix-vector multiplication, Liu and Vinter proposed new sparse matrix storing format CSR5 [15], a SIMD-friendly format for efficient computations of SpMV. Their approach can make SpMV kernel more SIMD friendly and ease to parallel and thus can gain performance speedup compared to MKL. They also developed CSR5-based SpMV algorithm on AMD and NVIDIA GPU which has better average performance than other existing formats. On the other hand, a thread-level parallel algorithm called merge-based SpMV [19] also claims to have great speedup for multi-core processors. BML [4] is an open source distributed library which supports for both dense and sparse matrix multiplication. They support for both ELLPACK and CSR format for sparse storage and implemented Gustavson algorithm as well as merge-based algorithm.

5.2 Performance Optimization Techniques on ARM

One optimization techniques on ARM architecture is tuning compilation flags as well as compiler itself to generate more efficient codes. Blackmore et al. [3] developed an auto-tuning method based on a collection of compilation flags used for GNU C compiler on ARM Cortex-M3 processor (CM3). They used a machine learning iterative method to obtain the optimal selections of optimization flags and finally gained two extra collections of compilation flags that outperforms standard *-O3* optimization for CM3 as well as AVR and CA8. On the other hand, Melnik et al. [18] made a case study on *libevas* to evaluate the impact of compiler optimization. They indicate the inefficiency of generated assembly code introduced by GCC's global common subexpression elimination (GCSE). They claim that original GCSE dose not aware whether the constant value will fit into ARM's 8 bit limited immediates. They also find that loop prefetching flags that show performance gains on ARMv6 architectures are not working well on ARMv8 based Cortex-A8 processor. They indicate that tuning with specific architecture's parameters for prefetching flags will gain as much as 20% performance gain in their evaluation.

Some other ARM-based optimization works are focused in the current ARM's many-core system as well as its SIMD unit called NEON. Bez et al. [1] performed HPC applications on ARMv8 Yggdrasil cluster and analyzed different optimization from time and energy aspects. They mainly reach performance gain from specific ARM compilation flags and NEON optimizations. Besides, Ruiz et al. [26] work on performance analysis and optimization of HPCG benchmark on ARM-based platform. In addition to applying optimal compilation flags and ARM-optimized math libraries, they also report multi-color reordering method and multi-block color reordering method to have less OpenMP thread synchronizations which will improve performance on current many-core ARM architecture. For ARMv8 based FTP processors, Chen et al. [5] benchmarked different formats of sparse matrix storage and developed a prediction model to choose an optimal format of sparse matrix storage of an unknown matrix. They claimed that NUMA-aware optimization on FTP can make notable speedup. They also claimed that vectorizing with NEON on ARMv8-based FTP led to performance loss since there were no efficient *gather* vector operations realized in ARMv8 architecture. Our work focuses on different architecture issues and gives some insights on future designs by benchmarking popular linear algebra kernels while they are interested in how different sparse matrix formats affect the performance on this specific architecture.

As ARM's low power and potentially high performance interest people to use in embedded systems as well as high-performance clusters, ARM developer releases collections of ARM performance libraries including BLAS, LAPACK, FFT and other commonly used math routines [8]. They officially claimed that their library's performance is better than widely-used OpenBLAS library. For machine learnings, they also developed a library called Compute Library [7] which targets Arm Cortex-A family of CPU processors and the Arm Mali family of GPUs. A case study [29] implements deep learning's embedded inference engine with Compute Library and they showed an overall speedup of 25% to Tensorflow.

6 Conclusion

In this paper, we evaluate the prototype Tianhe-3 cluster using representative linear algebra kernels with both dense and sparse datasets. The evaluation results are good performance indicators for assessing both the software and hardware designs as we are moving towards exascale. To better understand the evaluation results, we build roofline models for FTP and MTP processors that reveal the directions for future performance optimizations from the perspectives of both software developers and hardware architects. In addition, we compare the performance of FTP and MTP processors with Intel many-core KNL processor, which highlights the strengths and weaknesses among the architecture designs. We hope this paper can shed the lights on the path pursuing exascale supercomputers by taking the chance to report the work-in-progress of one of China exascale initiatives with Tianhe-3 for the HPC community. For the future work, we would like to compare with more architectures such as GPU and evaluate ARM high-performance libraries when they become available on FTP and MTP.

Acknowledgments. We would like to thank the National SuperComputer Center in Tianjin for offering us this opportunity to evaluate the prototype Tianhe-3 Cluster. This work is supported National Key R&D Program of China (Grant No. 2017YFB0202202) and National Natural Science Foundation of China (Grant No. 61502019).

References

1. Bez, J.L., Bernart, E.E., dos Santos, F.F., Schnorr, L.M., Navaux, P.O.A.: Performance and energy efficiency analysis of HPC physics simulation applications in a cluster of arm processors. Concurrency Comput.: Pract. Experience **29**(22), e4014 (2017)
2. Blackford, L.S., et al.: ScaLAPACK Users' Guide. SIAM, Philadelphia (1997)
3. Blackmore, C., Ray, O., Eder, K.: Automatically tuning the GCC compiler to optimize the performance of applications running on the ARM cortex-M3. CoRR (2017)
4. Bock, N., et al.: The basic matrix library (BML) for quantum chemistry. J. Supercomput. **74**(11), 6201–6219 (2018)
5. Chen, D., Fang, J., Chen, S., Xu, C., Wang, Z.: Optimizing sparse matrix-vector multiplications on an ARMv8-based many-core architecture. Int. J. Parallel Program. 1–15 (2018)
6. Davis, T.A., Hu, Y.: The university of florida sparse matrix collection. ACM Trans. Math. Softw. (TOMS) **38**(1), 1 (2011)
7. Arm Developer: Compute Library (2018). https://developer.arm.com/technologies/compute-library
8. ARM Developer: Arm performance libraries reference guide. ARM Developer (2018)
9. Dongarra, J.: Report on the TianHe-2a system. Technical report, ICL-UT-17-04, September 2017
10. FT-2000: Phytium Technology Co., Ltd. (2017). http://www.phytium.com.cn/Product/detail
11. hir0shim: Open source implentention of distributed SpMV on GitHuB (2015). https://github.com/hir0shim/distributedSpMV
12. Jacobsen, N.G., Fuhrman, D.R., Fredsøe, J.: A wave generation toolbox for the open-source CFD library: openfoam®. Int. J. Numer. Methods Fluids **70**(9), 1073–1088 (2012)
13. Krizhevsky, A., Sutskever, I., Hinton, G.E.: Imagenet classification with deep convolutional neural networks. In: Advances in Neural Information Processing Systems, pp. 1097–1105 (2012)
14. Langville, A.N., Meyer, C.D.: Google's PageRank and Beyond: The Science of Search Engine Rankings. Princeton University Press, Princeton (2011)
15. Liu, W., Vinter, B.: CSR5: an efficient storage format for cross-platform sparse matrix-vector multiplication. In: Proceedings of the 29th ACM on International Conference on Supercomputing, pp. 339–350. ACM (2015)
16. Liu, X., Smelyanskiy, M., Chow, E., Dubey, P.: Efficient sparse matrix-vector multiplication on x86-based many-core processors. In: Proceedings of the 27th International ACM Conference on International Conference on Supercomputing, pp. 273–282. ACM (2013)

17. McCalpin, J.D.: Stream benchmark, vol. 22 (1995). www.cs.virginia.edu/stream/ref.html#what
18. Melnik, D., Belevantsev, A., Plotnikov, D., Lee, S.: A case study: optimizing GCC on ARM for performance of libevas rasterization library. In: Proceedings of GROW (2010)
19. Merrill, D., Garland, M.: Merge-based parallel sparse matrix-vector multiplication. In: Proceedings of the International Conference for High Performance Computing, Networking, Storage and Analysis, p. 58. IEEE Press (2016)
20. Padoin, E.L., de Oliveira, D.A., Velho, P., Navaux, P.O.: Time-to-solution and energy-to-solution: a comparison between ARM and Xeon. In: 2012 Third Workshop on Applications for Multi-core Architectures (WAMCA), pp. 48–53. IEEE (2012)
21. Peise, E.: Performance modeling and prediction for dense linear algebra (2017). arXiv preprint arXiv:1706.01341
22. Plimpton, S., Crozier, P., Thompson, A.: Lammps-large-scale atomic/molecular massively parallel simulator. Sandia Nat. Laboratories **18**, 43 (2007)
23. Rajovic, N., et al.: The mont-blanc prototype: an alternative approach for HPC systems. In: International Conference for High Performance Computing, Networking, Storage and Analysis, SC 2016, pp. 444–455. IEEE (2016)
24. Rajovic, N., Rico, A., Puzovic, N., Adeniyi-Jones, C., Ramirez, A.: Tibidabo1: making the case for an ARM-based HPC system. Future Gener. Comput. Syst. **36**, 322–334 (2014)
25. Rajovic, N., Vilanova, L., Villavieja, C., Puzovic, N., Ramirez, A.: The low power architecture approach towards exascale computing. J. Comput. Sci. **4**(6), 439–443 (2013)
26. Ruiz, D., Mantovani, F., Casas, M., Labarta, J., Spiga, F.: The HPCG benchmark: analysis, shared memory preliminary improvements and evaluation on an arm-based platform (2018)
27. Shalf, J., Dosanjh, S., Morrison, J.: Exascale computing technology challenges. In: Palma, J.M.L.M., Daydé, M., Marques, O., Lopes, J.C. (eds.) VECPAR 2010. LNCS, vol. 6449, pp. 1–25. Springer, Heidelberg (2011). https://doi.org/10.1007/978-3-642-19328-6_1
28. Sodani, A.: Knights landing (KNL): 2nd generation Intel® Xeon Phi processor. In: 2015 IEEE, Hot Chips 27 Symposium (HCS), pp. 1–24. IEEE (2015)
29. Sun, D., Liu, S., Gaudiot, J.L.: Enabling embedded inference engine with arm compute library: a case study (2017). arXiv preprint arXiv:1704.03751
30. Szegedy, C., Ioffe, S., Vanhoucke, V., Alemi, A.A.: Inception-v4, inception-resnet and the impact of residual connections on learning. In: AAAI, vol. 4, p. 12 (2017)
31. Wang, E., et al.: Intel math kernel library. In: Wang, E., et al. (eds.) High-Performance Computing on the Intel® Xeon Phi™, pp. 167–188. Springer, Cham (2014). https://doi.org/10.1007/978-3-319-06486-4_7
32. Williams, S., Oliker, L., Vuduc, R., Shalf, J., Yelick, K., Demmel, J.: Optimization of sparse matrix-vector multiplication on emerging multicore platforms. In: Proceedings of the 2007 ACM/IEEE Conference on Supercomputing, SC 2007, pp. 1–12. IEEE (2007)
33. Williams, S., Waterman, A., Patterson, D.: Roofline: an insightful visual performance model for multicore architectures. Commun. ACM **52**(4), 65–76 (2009)
34. Xianyi, Z., Qian, W., Saar, W.: OpenBLAS: an optimized BLAS library (2016). http://www.openblas.net/. Accessed 12 May 2016
35. Zhang, C.: Mars: a 64-core ARMv8 processor. In: 2015 IEEE Hot Chips 27 Symposium (HCS), pp. 1–23. IEEE (2015)

Author Index

www.ingramcontent.com/pod-product-compliance
Lightning Source LLC
LaVergne TN
LVHW082239200926
848484LV00008B/2377
9781013271199